KILLER WEATHER

KILLER WEATHER

STORIES OF GREAT DISASTERS

HOWARD E.
SMITH, JR.

DODD, MEAD & COMPANY
New York

1 2 3 4 5 6 7 8 9 10

Library of Congress Cataloging in Publication Data

Smith, Howard Everett
  Killer weather.

  Bibliography: p.
  Includes index.
  1. Storms—United States—Popular works. 2. United States—Climate—Popular works. 3. Natural disasters—United States—Popular works. 4. Weather—Popular works.
I. Title
QC943.5.U6S63   973   81-22114
ISBN 0-396-08055-3   AACR2

For
Grand-mère,
who did so much

Contents

List of Illustrations

Introduction

For most of us, weather is normally something that just happens, something that hardly bothers us. Rarely are we concerned about it, beyond finding out whether or not we need an umbrella, overcoat and scarf, or seersucker for the day.

But aside from wars, the worst disasters by far are caused by severe weather conditions. Hurricanes have destroyed towns. Long, cold summers have ruined vital crops. Floods have destroyed factories and cities and left thousands homeless. Severe droughts have killed hundreds of thousands of people and left devastation.

America has its share of killer weather and then some. We have the worst tornadoes and the greatest number of them. The severest of blizzards have swept through our states. Hurricanes packing fierce winds have ravaged American seacoasts. We have suffered from droughts such as the one that caused the Dust Bowl, disrupting the lives of over a million Americans and bringing about profound social, economic, and political changes. We also suffered through "the year without a summer."

Weather can be unbelievably dangerous at times. This book describes killer weather in many of its forms, and it tells of the heroism of people caught up in terrible circumstances beyond their control. Many have been called upon to function at a superhuman level when their world is falling apart around them. Mothers save children. Fathers protect families. In some cases, a child, all alone, survives under hellish conditions.

We humans are tough. It is impossible even to imagine a situation so horrible, so terrible, or so dangerous that some person has not already faced in reality. Fact, in this sense, is far more unusual than fiction. No novelist could ever have dreamed up the escapes some people have made, nor their inventive ways of surviving great catastrophes.

Killer weather is part of the human condition, part of what we may at any time have to deal with. It is to give an insight into this human condition that I have undertaken to record here these great stories and the stories of the people who have seen and suffered in killer weather.

But I also mean this book to serve another function. In learning about these storms and droughts we will come to know a bit more about their nature. That will make it possible for us all to be better prepared for similar natural disasters. It is those who are most prepared who, statistically speaking, are most likely to survive disaster. Those who understand the nature of violent storms and who take storm warnings seriously have the best chance of making it through.

Some people mistakenly believe that radar, satellite photographs, airplane patrols, computers, and the like can protect us from every violent storm. It is certainly true that modern science has saved countless thousands of lives from being lost in hurricanes, tornadoes, blizzards, and other severe weather conditions. There can be no question about that.

On the other hand, the population is growing everywhere. This forces people to live in areas susceptible to hazardous flooding, to commute on dangerously exposed highways. Because of such factors, violent storms take a high toll of life each year. And there is always the possibility of greater disaster in the future, especially in urban areas. Droughts have become progressively worse in terms of deaths occasioned because there are more people than ever in the world and almost every available productive acre on this planet is growing food. Some scientists believe it is only a matter of time before a catastrophic drought takes place that will have a worldwide impact, even affecting the so-called developed nations.

In addition to all this, some killer weather is manmade. Humans are, for example, solely responsible for killer smogs. Poor land management can turn a drought into a disaster. No one knows what the long-term effect of carbon-dioxide pollution in the air will be. Could it heat up the atmosphere so much that worldwide droughts occur? Could industrial dusts in the air bring about a worldwide cooling effect? Is it possible that in spite of science, the worst is yet to come? Or does the progress of science itself expose us to greater dangers? Like many things, science is a two-edged sword.

We should never tell ourselves we are perfectly safe, for we never really can be. The greatest danger is complacency. We must live with the weather. In fact, we are alive because rains fall on our crops and fill our reservoirs. We survive because the sun shines on us and allows us to live healthy lives. We need changes in weather for our psychological well-being. We need the winds, for they pollinate plants, mix the oxygen in proper ways, carry away pollution. Odd as it may seem, we even need hurricanes, for they play an important role in bringing needed moisture from the tropics to the temperate zones.

In numerous ways we are part of the weather. Changing weather patterns give us our life, even though at times, severe weather can kill us. There is no human realm other than this planet, with its land, sea, and atmosphere. The sunlight and rain are as much a part of us as our heart, kidneys, and liver. We live in a complex environment that sustains us but can also kill us.

KILLER WEATHER

1. The Northeast Blizzard of 1888

Saturday, March 10, 1888, was, by all accounts, a glorious day: mild and partly sunny. The sun itself had a springlike haze and softness to it. New Yorkers were thinking of spring. People sat out on stoops and basked in the sun, planning Easter costumes or thinking about what seeds to buy for their window flower boxes. Boys in the streets tossed balls back and forth and talked and joked about the coming baseball season. No one that day had an inkling that the worst storm in New York's history was brewing.

In spite of the warm weather, a blizzard of unprecedented proportions was in the making. Huge amounts of moisture were moving up the eastern seaboard from the Gulf of Mexico. In fact, the warm weather of Saturday was part of that system. But to the northwest, an air mass of bitterly cold Canadian arctic air was moving over the almost uninhabited parts of Manitoba and Ontario. The moist Gulf air and the cold arctic air were on a collision course. All the classical ingredients of a huge blizzard were there. What happens in all blizzards was happening. The warm, moist air rode up over the cold air. The moisture rapidly condensed, and rain began to fall. As there are no references to thunder and lightning that I know of, it seems probable that at first the warm air mass near the seaboard moved toward the polar air mass and gently slipped over the cold front. For a while the warm, tropical air mass pushed the polar air mass backward. As it did so, the warm air rose higher and cooled off very rapidly. Before long snow was falling.

The temperature difference between the two air masses was enormous. The warm air mass had temperatures in the sixties. The temperatures in the polar air mass were subzero at ground level and even colder higher up. The warm air mass had a great deal of moisture in it, and the cold air rapidly condensed that.

Early in the storm the warm air mass continued to make headway against the cold air mass. But sometime during the night the polar air mass pushed the warm air mass back. The front where the two met lay along the eastern seaboard from about western Massachusetts to Washington, D.C. That defined the area that would get the heaviest snowfall. The polar air mass gathered strength, in terms of wind and southward movement. At the worst of the storm the polar air mass was moving at about 80 miles an hour toward the southeast, which is extraordinarily fast, making the violence of the storm very unusual.

North America is an excellent breeding grounds for blizzards. In part this is due to the shape of the continent. The northernmost part of it is much wider than its southern part, around Mexico. In the huge area of the Arctic just below the North Pole, cold air masses reach temperatures of $-70°$F. On the other hand, air masses that develop in the Gulf of Mexico and Atlantic Ocean even in the winter may have a temperature of as much as $+60°$F.

Since polar air masses will eventually move south, and tropical, marine air masses will eventually move north, blizzards are bound to happen. In the United States, most occur in the Dakotas and other parts of the Midwest. It was somewhat unusual for the two air masses that caused the blizzard of 1888 to be so far east. Blizzards do in fact hit the region at least once every decade, but the blizzard of 1888 is by far the worst on record.

The U.S. Weather Bureau (as it was then called) knew something of the conditions, but because so few stations in Canada were reporting them, and because knowledge of the movement of air masses was so sketchy then, the bureau predicted only light snows for Sunday. Not one meteorologist mentioned the possibility of a blizzard.

Rain fell on Sunday, instead of the predicted snow. At first it was a light rain, but as the day wore on, it became heavier. For a while there was a real downpour. Several areas were flooded. Storm sewers backed up. After nightfall temperatures plummeted. At the same time, the winds increased. All night the storm gathered momentum.

The first to experience the storm's intensity were sailors at sea. During the night the sea became incredibly rough. Howling winds filled the air with blinding spray. Waves crashed against ships. A large luxury yacht, the *Cythera,* struggled in the seas and then sank. All aboard drowned. Almost one hundred ships and boats caught in Chesapeake Bay by the sudden storm were lost. Thirty-seven boats were sunk or battered beyond repair in Delaware Bay. The logs of ocean-going liners reveal that the waves at sea were huge and dangerous. Even the largest, strongest steamers were shipping green water.

At sea near New York Harbor, and in the harbor itself, ships were having a terrible time of it. Even sturdy pilot boats were in danger. (Pilot boats are extremely seaworthy boats that carry pilots in incoming ships to guide them through the harbor to their docks. They also pick up pilots from ships heading out to sea.)

By coincidence, reporter William Inglis of the *New York World* had decided to do a feature article about life aboard a New York pilot boat. On Saturday he had boarded Pilot Boat No. 13. During the night hurricane winds nearly sank it off Sandy Hook. The waves were so huge that the hull of the boat disappeared time and again under tons of water. Unhappy, seasick Inglis had more of a story than he had bargained for. Several times the boat almost capsized. The strain on the hull was so great that the boat sprang several leaks. All night and through the next day the pumps were manned. The boat should have been brought in, but the captain, knowing it might get battered against a dock and sink, decided to keep it in open water. After a twenty-four-hour battle against the storm the ship landed safely. Inglis, who probably never wanted to set foot on another boat as long as he lived, went ashore with quite a story. He must have considered himself a very lucky man. Thirty-three ships sank in New York Harbor that day.

Few people in New York City knew of the storm during its first hours. The wind rose while they slept. Around midnight, the rain turned to snow. Howling winds drove the snow across rooftops. Flooded areas quickly turned to ice. Before dawn the temperature was well below zero. When people woke up, there was already deep snow on the ground. The city was in the grips of a raging blizzard. Considering the date, many people must have been astonished.

The wisest people rolled over, snuggled down, and went right back to sleep. As it turned out, those who stayed home were the most fortunate. But most workers donned heavy overcoats, hats, scarves, and boots to brave the elements.

At that time one and a half million people lived in America's largest city. New York was considered the glory of the New World, the most modern city of its time. It prided itself on its splendid communications and transportation systems, without doubt the best in the world. Countless thousands of miles of telephone and telegraph lines connected it to all the states and every corner of the globe. All sorts of up-to-date transportation was available: railroad trains, elevated railroads, horse-drawn railroads, cabs, coaches, and other horse-drawn vehicles. Boats plied the harbor, and ferries connected Manhattan with Brooklyn and Staten Island. The Brooklyn Bridge, a marvel of engineering for that time, spanned the East River. Within hours both the communications and transportation systems would be either in shambles or not operating.

By early morning it was already too dangerous to cross the harbor in ferries. In those days no subways connected Brooklyn with Manhattan, so people went either by ferry or crossed the Brooklyn Bridge. But no one crossed the bridge on the day of the blizzard. The cables were coated with ice, and winds over 80 miles per hour were sweeping over it. Snow fell across it in waves of white so that the great towers were not visible. The temperature was below zero. The few policemen who went out on it were forced back. Early in the morning authorities closed the bridge.

The communications system fared no better. Within hours howling winds driving snow against the telegraph, telephone, and electrical wires, which then hung between poles, coated them with ice. Wires began to snap in the gusts of wind, and poles fell to the ground. Live wires, a dangerous threat to pedestrians and horses, lay hidden in the snow. Anyone stepping on them could be electrocuted. And so, early in the morning the great communications system began to fail. Important news could neither enter nor leave the city. For several days New Yorkers had little news about what was happening outside the city: about lost trains, about blocked roads, about ships at sea, and all the rest of it. In addition, the broken electrical lines blacked out many sections of the city. All through the storm power failures increased. Perhaps worst of all, the alarm boxes used to notify fire departments stopped working. All day gale-force winds whipped through the city; all day the damage spread.

People trying to go to work were blinded by clouds of snow blowing in their faces. The *New York Times* described the winds as a strange combination of force coming from one direction, yet simultaneously having a rotary motion. These winds confused anyone on the streets. And there were other problems. Signs fell; awnings caved in; tree branches crashed to the ground. There was danger at every turn.

Early-morning commuters were still able to get rides on the elevated trains. Others found horse-drawn transportation. But those few who got to work found that offices and factories were mostly vacant. Many businesses were manned by only a few workers. Most businesses remained shuttered. The New York Stock Exchange, however, did open, but only thirty-three employees out of eleven hundred arrived that morning. Because the ticker tape was controlled by telegraphic means, it barely operated. Most of the senior officials, who alone were authorized to endorse checks and sell stocks, did not arrive at their offices. Throughout the city, key bank officers were also missing from their offices. At noon the few officials who had made it there simply gave up and closed the stock exchange. It was the first time since its beginning in 1790 that weather had shut it down.

By noon the city was almost unrecognizable. Familiar landmarks had taken on weird aspects. The facade of Trinity Church looked like a surrealistic piece of art. Twisted snow forms clung to it. Icy gargoyles stared at passersby. Huge icicle stalactites hung in beautiful shapes from eaves and cornices. Trinity Church was not an isolated case. Many buildings looked like images out of dreams. The city had never been so fascinatingly beautiful, but it had never been so cruelly inhospitable either.

In the early afternoon, the blizzard was worse. Three and a

half feet of snow had already fallen, and more was coming down, Eighteen-foot-high drifts were common. Snowdrifts halted all transportation, aside from a few horse-drawn vehicles operated by cabbies; some of whom were charging people forty dollars to go a mile. Others charged a dollar a block. Only the very wealthy could afford to ride at these prices. Everyone else had to walk.

But to walk was to take your life in your hands. One who walked was Harold Osterman. He struggled through the blizzard and reported that the snow was flying in all directions. Most of the time he could see nothing ahead of himself. At times, he and another pedestrian would bump into each other and, like tops, spin away after colliding. At other times, the wind itself would actually set him twirling. The sidewalks were so slippery from the ice below the snow that he was forced to walk in the middle of the street.

As he walked he tripped over something and fell into the soft snow. He was so exhausted from his efforts that he just lay where he was for several moments to rest. But he knew that there was a great danger in doing that. Moreover, he became curious about what he had just tripped over. He stood up and searched for the object. Then he saw what it was. *It* was two boots sticking out of the snow. He pulled on them. There was a man attached to them. He dragged the body out of the snow, kneeled, and looked down. He was staring into the face of a dead man—rigid and white blotched with blue. The man's mouth was partly open and his teeth could be seen, slightly parted. His eyes were frozen to ice.

Osterman, shaken by the sight, looked for a policeman. He could not see one anywhere. He went to find one. Then he realized his own danger. If he searched too long for a policeman, he himself would be lying dead in the snow. As quickly as he could, he headed for home. It was a terrible struggle floundering through the ever deepening snow. Fortunately, he reached his apartment building. He went into his bedroom so tired he could hardly get undressed. For over twelve hours he lay in a deep sleep. When he woke up he wondered about the dead man. He never learned who that man was, but the face haunted him for the rest of his life.

A great many people fainted from cold on the streets. All during the blizzard, policemen dragged people to cover. Twenty Brooklyn mailmen were discovered unconscious in the snow. They were saved. Policemen were sent to unheated apartments to bring people into the police stations, where they could get warm. Given the terrible conditions they faced, the policemen did a remarkable job. Countless numbers were saved by them. But they did not find everyone in time.

One who did not escape death in the blizzard was George D. Bareman, who died trying to get to his downtown office. He tried to take the elevated, as he always did, but a policeman informed him that it was closed due to the storm. He told Bareman that another elevated three blocks away was still working. Bareman was last seen walking toward it. He never made it. A few hours later two policemen found his frozen body at Seventh Avenue and 54th Street.

Many others died of heart failure. They frequently died hours, even days, after their struggle with the snow. One of those who died that way was Senator Roscoe Conkling. He left his Wall Street office and set off for the New York Club. Unable to find any moving transportation, he walked. At Union Square he started to walk over a snowdrift. He thought he could just walk over the top of it, but when he got onto the middle of it, he began to sink. Deeper and deeper he went. His feet could not find bottom, and he was soon swimming in the snow.

He could have called for help, but it would have done no good. No one in that howling wind could hear him. He fought and swam and struggled. He was sure he was trapped and that he would expire there, but by using every ounce of his energies he managed to extricate himself from the drift. By then his clothes were covered with ice. He walked on until he arrived at the club. Amazingly he made it, but he was done in. Shaking, frozen, totally exhausted, he ordered a drink. As he sipped it, he fell into a delirium. He was placed in a bed. The next day he was dead. As the *New York Times* asked editorially, "How many lives will be shortened by the blizzard?" We will never know, but we can guess that many people died earlier than they otherwise would have because of it.

In every disaster there are nevertheless a few comic stories. One man, C. H. McDonald, was floundering through a big drift when his head hit something. He received a nasty gash and was bleeding badly. Upon looking, McDonald found to his amazement that his head had collided with the hoof of a dead horse. Instead of being upset or angered, he laughingly told all his friends he was the only man ever to be kicked in the head by a dead horse.

By mid-afternoon there were thousands of abandoned vehicles in the streets and numerous dead horses. Because of the danger to their steeds, many cabbies, draymen, wagoners, and others unhitched their horses and rode them to the nearest stable where they could get shelter. They were fearful that the strain of dragging wagons, carriages, or other vehicles through the snow would kill or injure the horses. They were also fearful that the cold weather itself would harm them.

The streets were a white hell. Live electrical wires hung down, broken signs with dangerous sharp metal edges or splinters of wood, telephone poles, and other similar objects lay hidden under the snow ready to injure anyone. In addition to all that were the abandoned vehicles, dead horses, and an occasional dead pedestrian.

The people on the elevated trains fared no better. By early afternoon not one train worked anymore. In all of the great city not one moved. Most stalled far from any station. People found themselves trapped high above the streets. There was no way to get down. It was a terrible situation. The wind howled, and temperatures inside the cars dropped way below freezing. Some enterprising people saw a good way to make a fast buck. They placed rickety tall ladders up against the trains and charged people twenty dollars to escape. Others got hot soup for the stranded passengers and charged them two dollars a bowl. It was piracy. The trapped people often had no choice but to pay to be rescued.

A few frightened passengers had to cross on "bridges" made of ladders and poles placed three or four stories above the street. These bridges spanned the space between a train and the upper windows of a building next to the elevated tracks. People crawling over them nearly passed out from fear. The memory of these experiences was one factor that subsequently spurred city officials into deciding to concentrate on the development of subway trains.

Other trains were having a time of it, too. Of the forty trains scheduled to come into the city that day, only two made it. On all the lines for miles around there were stranded trains. In some cases frozen switches stopped them. In most cases, it was the drifts that had stalled them. From Philadelphia, Boston, and Albany, trains headed for New York City were sitting in the cold wind, being covered with drifts. Since most of the telegraph lines were down, railroad officials had no idea where the trains were. Many were simply lost. No one knew where to search for them. The trains just sat.

Conditions inside the trains were frightful. It was so cold that the water froze in the lines. Sanitary facilities were not working. Worse, there was no drinking water. Many of the passengers and crew who had to wait for up to two days for rescue suffered terribly. Because of the cold, passengers broke up furniture inside the trains and burned it in the wood-burning stoves. Odd as it may seem, many who were later rescued said their worst problem was boredom. Some sat in their seats and stared at the white snow outside all day, all night, and through another day.

By 3:00 P.M. Grand Central Terminal was closed. It was obvious by then that no train was going to arrive. It must have been an eerie place. The station at that time had a very high glass ceiling. Snow blew down the tracks and then swept upward in the huge room. It went all the way up to the glass ceiling and then spiraled down again. It looked as though it was actually snowing inside. Everything in the immense room was covered with snow.

People who were on stranded trains had two choices. They could sit in the cold, uncomfortable cars and get hungrier and thirstier by the hour, or they could brave the storm and walk through it to a town, cafe, or hotel nearby or make a trek across country to a farm. Most wisely stayed on the trains.

One train caught in the storm was the New York Central *Flyer,* which had left Buffalo, New York, for New York City at 5:00 P.M. Sunday, March 11. Outside of Albany, the train's engineer saw mountainous snowdrifts ahead. He decided that by getting up enough power, he could ram the huge steam engine, weighing over one hundred tons, right through them. He stopped the train, backed it up, and headed down the track again at the drifts. Faster and faster the train went. The huge wheels thundered on the tracks. As the locomotive hit the drift, huge sprays of snow spurted into the air. It looked as if the train would smash through the drifts. But the train jolted to a sudden halt. As it did so, hot coals spilled out of a stove, and in a few minutes a car was on fire. The snowdrifts now held the locomotive in a viselike grip.

Alarmed by the smell of smoke, the passengers, who were actually in no danger, decided to leave. Among them was seventeen-year old Sarah Wilson. Together with the others, she stepped off the train into the blizzard. Swirling clouds of snow raced past. Their feet sunk down into the drifts. They walked together, but were blinded by the howling, snow-filled wind. Somehow the passengers, holding on to each other, lost Sarah. She walked off alone. Blinded by the snow, she probably lost her way. Finally too cold and numb to go on, she lay down, never to rise again.

Other passengers in other trains, seeing nearby farmhouses, left the shelter of their trains to walk to them. Many died. Some were not found until later in the spring, when the thawing snow-drifts exposed their bodies.

As the snows progressively became deeper, New York City became more paralyzed. There were no food deliveries and milk was unobtainable. Medical supplies ran low, and many people had to forego their daily drugs. Stores were, for the most part, closed. Those few that opened were run by skeleton crews.

By 5:00 P.M., when it was time to go home, many wondered what to do. Few dared venture out at all. Cautious workers slept in factories, shops, and offices. It was safer to curl up on a floor and get a rotten night's sleep than venture out. Those who had money headed for downtown hotels. These were soon packed. Hotel owners, seeing a chance for gouging, raised prices five times above normal. Restaurants did a booming business. With supplies low, they could get away with skyrocketing prices. Every bar in town was filled with people. The customers no doubt felt that a wee bit o' whiskey would take the chill out of their blood. Due to the huge crowds, most bars soon ran out of liquor.

As night came on, the storm finally began to let up. Fifty inches of snow had fallen. Most of it had not stayed on roofs, but had blown down into the streets. Huge drifts twenty, thirty, forty, even fifty feet high loomed up in the streets and against buildings. The greatest city in the western hemisphere, para-lyzed that night, looked eerie. Hardly a soul dared to walk about. Never had the streets been so desolate, so empty, so white. Very few street lamps cast any light on that snow.

A great blizzard can easily cripple a city as one did in Hamburg, New York, on February 2, 1977. Drifts similar to these covered much of New York City during the blizzard of 1888. *National Oceanic and Atmospheric Administration*

Because of breakages in the wires, most of the city was blacked out. What a strange place. Manhattan belonged wholly to the mournful wind moaning down the masonry canyons.

At the New York City Weather Bureau, meteorologists were trying to make sense of it all. They came up with some amazing figures. At its worst, the temperature had gone below zero degrees Fahrenheit. The highest wind speeds were unknown, because wind-speed instruments broke down at the height of the storm. Naturally, the meteorologists were upset by this. With the biggest storm in the city's history howling outside their windows, they had no idea how fast the wind was blowing.

The instruments, all jammed, were on top of a pole 150 feet above the street. To go up there in the storm to repair them was madness. Yet one man decided to brave the storm and do just that. He was Francis Long, who had been a member of the famous Adolphus Greely expedition to the arctic. He decided to shinny up the pole and get the instruments working. He started up. The pole bent in the wind. Long was whipped back and forth as, inch by inch, he went up the pole. People watching him held their breath. At the top of the pole he brushed away the snow and cut the ice away from the instruments—the anemometer started turning again. Unfortunately, he got them going after the highest gust had swept through the city. Nevertheless, the instruments recorded wind speeds of up to 75 miles per hour, hurricane force. No one knows the speed during the height of the storm, but most evidence shows that gusts were hitting well over 80 miles per hour, and perhaps higher. It was very difficult to determine how much snow fell. The best estimate is that in New York City between forty and fifty inches fell. There were huge drifts everywhere. One drift at Gravesend was fifty-two feet high.

New Yorkers were convinced that the worst of the storm was centered on New York City itself. Part of this was pure provincialism. Part of it was due to the fact that news could not spread, for the telephone and telegraph lines were down from Philadelphia to Boston and from New York to Albany. In Middletown, Connecticut, more than fifty inches of snow fell. There were drifts over sixty feet high in parts of western Massachusetts and in Connecticut. People could only go in and out of their houses through long tunnels dug in the snow. There were some freak accidents outside of New York because of the depth of the snow. One involved some coal barges being towed up the Hudson River. A load of snow built up on the coal and in the barges as a tugboat pulled them. Finally there was so much snow that the barges sank from the weight of it.

After the snow stopped falling, the city began to dig out. On Tuesday, March 13, 1888, the *New York Times* bemoaned the economic loss to the city. An article stated that the fact that businesses had shut down and that factories had been closed would hurt wage earners. Actually, the opposite happened for most laborers. In those days the city had no snow-removal equipment. Labor was at a premium. Men with shovels could ask for and get high wages. Able-bodied men had never had it so good. Armies of highly paid men began to clean up the city, so that supplies such as badly needed milk and other critical goods could get into the city as rapidly as possible.

As the men with shovels tackled the drifts, they occasionally came upon the bodies of pedestrians. One was the body of a frozen boy, estimated to be twelve years old. He had no identification on him at all. For days the newspapers and city made a plea for anyone knowing him to identify him. No one ever came forth. Finally he was given an unknown's funeral, which was well attended by those saddened by his lonely death.

All up and down the seacoast bodies rolled in with the tides. A few drifts in New England did not completely melt away until mid-June. Every now and then one would give up a body. The official death toll was put at four hundred dead. The figure, of course, is a mere estimate. No one really knows how many died—how many never rolled ashore, how many decayed in areas away from any habitation. However, four hundred is probably close to the mark.

2. The Year without a Summer

Who has not wondered some cold day in spring whether summer will ever arrive? All of us at some time must have wondered if there was ever a year when summer never arrived. In fact there was. The year 1816 has gone down in history as the year without a summer. Snow fell in June, July, and August in New England and eastern Canada. It was the coldest summer on record in parts of England and western Europe.

The cold summer arrived unannounced. The winter of 1815–16 in New England and eastern Canada had been normal in every respect. Like most winters in that region, it had been snowy, cold, and blustery, but it was neither colder nor snowier than normal. April was also normal.

It was warm on May 1. Records show that in New Haven and Hartford, Connecticut; Williamstown, Massachusetts; and Brunswick, Maine, the temperature was above normal that day. It stayed on the warm side until May 5. Then the temperature took a nose dive. Day by day until May 13 it progressively got lower. By then it was 17 degrees below normal.

Farmers who had just finished their spring planting of corn were surprised to see their fields covered with a coating of white frost. None of them had seen frost that late in the year. It was almost three weeks after the average date that the last killing frost normally occurred. As farmers walked in their fields, they could see their breath. Plants were blackened by the frost. Recently planted corn was threatened, and the farmers' livelihood was in jeopardy. But there was nothing they could do but go back in their houses, have a cup of tea, warm up, and hope that seasonable weather would return.

The weather changed, and it did warm up. From May 18 until May 20 the temperature climbed upward. On the twentieth the mean temperature (that is to say, the midpoint between the highest and lowest temperatures for the day) was 74°F in Hartford, Connecticut. That was a record high for a mean temperature for that city on that day. It was warm all through New England, and for the next three days it stayed warmer than normal throughout those states.

New hope rose in the hearts of the farmers. The cold wave of early and mid-May was now like a half-recalled nightmare. It had obviously been some sort of freak occurrence that would not happen again.

But the warm weather did not last. A week later frost again covered the fields in many parts of New England. Farmers could hardly believe the hoary white landscape that greeted their eyes. This cold wave lasted until June first. A warm spell followed. From June 1 to June 5 the temperatures throughout New England were above average. No one knew what to make of all this. New England was known for its changeable weather, but this was truly bizarre. During the warm spell farmers kept their fingers crossed.

Then disaster hit. On June 5 a bitterly cold wind swept across eastern Canada and New England. With it came a blizzard. That really amazed and frightened farmers. It was like winter.

They bundled up in coats, scarves, wool hats, mittens, and winter boots and went out to assess the damage. Crops stood frozen black in front of their eyes. Worst hit was the corn. It wilted away in the freezing winds. Many trees lost their leaves. Dead birds were seen throughout the fields. In Canada ice thickened on ponds, trapping and killing large flocks of ducks.

People simply could not believe it. The region had been settled for almost two centuries, and no one could recall any stories or legends of a blizzard in June. It was unheard of.

The *North Star,* a local newspaper in Danville, Vermont, noted in the understated language typical of that time, "Probably no one living in the country ever witnessed such weather, especially of so long continuance."

Those farmers who had planted corn suffered a complete loss of their crops. But they were not totally without hope. They figured that if the weather warmed up again, they could plant once more. With a little luck they could still get in a crop of corn before autumn. The temperature slowly rose again. Farmers planted corn and hoped for the best. By June 21 the temperatures were again above normal. In New Haven it was about 90°F—hot and muggy. Farmers throughout New England were convinced the worst was over. They figured that now the temperature would hold. But it did not.

On July 4 the whole eastern seaboard was in the grip of yet another cold wave. The highest temperature recorded in Savannah, Georgia, that day was only 46°F. There were fields in the heart of the South that were white with frost on Independence Day.

Many farmers tried to fight back. During the nights of early July they burned their hay. All through New England one could see bonfires glowing in the fields. Weary, frightened farm families stayed up all night to tend them. It was a desperate situation. The farmers, most of whom were quite poor, were burning valuable hay that could always be sold or used for their own livestock. It was like burning money to keep alive. This action did save some corn. Here and there a few fields of corn in well-protected areas also survived. But the losses in corn crops were huge.

As often happens, fundamentalist preachers began to tell their congregations that God was punishing them for their sins. Others called it a prelude to Doomsday. Since most New Englanders were from Puritan stock, many believed this. Special prayer meetings were held throughout the region. People all around wondered what it meant on a cosmic scale.

On a cosmic scale, the cold was very limited. Only eastern Canada, New England, occasionally some of the rest of the eastern seaboard, and western Europe suffered from the exceptional cold that summer.

In a day of limited communication, the average New Englander did not know how widespread the cold might be. Those listening to the fundamentalists probably thought the whole world had cooled down. Others, not knowing about the cold weather in western Europe, probably considered it just a local weather phenomenon. However, Geneva, Switzerland, and parts of England such as the Lancaster Plain were experiencing the coldest summers since records had been kept there.

The cold weather once more loosened its grip on New England. The temperature shot upward to above normal for two days: July 13 and July 14. What a roller-coaster summer. Up and down the temperature went, hitting record lows some weeks and going above normal other days.

Farmers felt that they had one more chance to get in a corn crop. It was a slim chance and they knew it, but they gambled that the weather would hold through August and that there would be just enough warm days in September so that crops could ripen. Once more they planted corn.

The weather held through early August. By mid-August the temperature throughout New England was above normal. The corn thrived in the heat. In the warm wind, farmers once more heard the wonderful sound of rustling, growing leaves. Farm families worked long hours in the fields in an effort to tend the valuable crop. From dawn to dusk they pulled weeds, put up scarecrows, and did everything possible to hasten the growth of the corn. By August 20 there was a feeling of hope. Many plants had ears of corn, which were rapidly ripening.

Then on August 21 the final disaster hit. The temperature rapidly fell. A heavy snow fell in the hills and mountains of New England. That snow would lay on the ground until the next summer. White frost covered the fields. It was the worst frost ever seen in August. A cold wind swept the land. Women who hung wet laundry in the morning gathered stiff, frozen clothes in the afternoon. Field hands could see their breath. Though it was August, men worked in heavy coats and wore mittens and had their caps pulled down over their ears.

As for the corn, there was nothing to do but to gather the ears and try to dry the kernels that might be ripe. Perhaps these could be saved as feed for animals. But none of the corn was ripe enough to dry correctly, so it rotted. At such a late date, there was no sense even trying to plant another crop. New England had lost most of its corn crop for 1816.

About the only good thing that could be said about the cold weather that summer was that it had killed countless billions of mosquitoes. Each time they started to hatch, they were frozen to death. For once, New Englanders were not bothered by the usual summer clouds of mosquitoes. But not only the mosquitoes died. So did most insects. Columbia College had made out a contract with an entomologist who was to go to New England that summer to collect insects for the natural history department's collection. He could not find enough insects to fulfill his contract. He wrote the college and complained about the lack of them.

Before the year ended, several researchers collected facts

about the summer. Members of the Philadelphia Society for the Promotion of Agriculture were very curious to know exactly what had happened in terms of farm crops, farm prices, and so on. They sent questionnaires to farmers all over the northeast. Through this method, they found out that half of the corn crop on New York's Long Island had been destroyed. Three-fourths of the corn crop of New England had been destroyed. Only half the usual amount of hay was grown. Oddly, the hay that did survive was considered superior to the hay gathered most years. Wheat and rye did well; so did root crops.

Since corn was the major New England crop, 1816 was a disastrous year. Because corn failed, prices for all grains and hay rose sharply. The price of wheat doubled in the next year; and the price of hay skyrocketed. Normally it sold for $30 per ton. By 1817 it was going for $180 per ton. Many farmers, unable to feed their cattle or pigs, slaughtered them. The price of meat fell because so many were killed. Pork, which sold for around $24 a barrel most of the time, went for $17 a barrel in the fall of 1816.

There are many accounts of suicides. It has been said that numerous farmers hanged themselves, but this is probably a great exaggeration. It is doubtful the suicide rate ever went up. On the other hand, many farmers did leave their land. Records show that in 1816 and 1817 twice as many people left Vermont and New Hampshire as in 1815. Many others who did not actually leave New England probably flocked to the cities and took poor-paying jobs in textile mills. Those who stayed on the farm must have been fearful about 1817. Would it too be a year without a summer?

For all their suffering, the New Englanders were not the worst off. Eastern Canada suffered a greater disaster by far. Americans, at the worst, only lost corn and hay. The eastern Canadians lost those crops and the valuable wheat crop. The cold winds, sleet, and blizzards that swept across the eastern provinces that summer did tremendous damage to all crops. The unseasonal cold also destroyed huge quantities of wildlife of all types. The *Halifax Weekly Chronicle* stated that "a great distress prevails throughout Quebec Province from a scarcity of food. Bread and milk is the common food of the poorer classes at this season of the year; but many have no bread."

As bad as it was in North America, it was nothing compared to western Europe. The cold summer and consequent crop failures were devastating to areas that had not yet fully recovered from the Napoleonic wars. Although conflict officially ended in 1815, the economies were still geared for war. Factories that had produced guns had not yet changed over to the production of farm equipment—the swords had not yet been beaten into plowshares. Far from it. Most farmers lacked even basic equipment. In addition, men needed to till the land were dead or injured. Others had not returned home. The farm economy could not have been worse. Even if normally warm weather had arrived during the summer of 1816, crop yield would have been marginal. The last thing needed was a disastrously cold summer that destroyed crops.

By the end of the summer, grain was in such short supply that tens of thousands of Europeans hunted in the woods for wild plants to eat. Like packs of wild animals, groups searched for anything to put in their mouths. So many mistook poisonous plants for edible plants that local officials, fearing more deaths, ordered pamphlets describing poisonous plants printed so people could identify and avoid them. But great numbers of people could not even forage for food. They began to die of starvation by the thousands. Churches designated January 26, 1817, as a day of prayer and made a plea for funds to feed the the starving. Death rates naturally rise when there is widespread malnutrition. European records show that the death rate during the winter of 1816–17 soared.

In France, things were completely out of hand. When the

government placed a three-franc tax on every bushel of imported wheat, riots broke out in Poitiers. Troops marched against rioters. During midsummer, farm wagons loaded with anything edible could not move from French farms to towns or cities without the protection of troops. Roving bands of hungry people regularly attacked such wagons to steal what food they could. As a result, many farmers decided against sending any food to market. Of course, this only made things worse. In the Loire Valley a huge mob of over two thousand people fought troops in an effort to get to wagons carrying grain. By the end of the summer, the French government, which had tried to stop the importation of grain in order to encourage domestic production reversed itself and removed all taxes on grain to encourage foreign supplies. Fearing widespread rebellion, even civil war, it had no other choice. Conditions remained desperate until the harvest of 1817 brought down the price of grain and bread. But during the latter part of 1816 and early 1817 nightmarish hunger conditions prevailed in western Europe because of the summer's cold weather.

Though many in North America and western Europe feared the summer of 1817 would bring further calamity or even the end of the world, the summer of 1817 was normal. In fact, no summer on record before or since 1816 has been so cold.

The question that of course arises is: What caused the cold weather?

At the time no one had a clue as to its cause. We can well imagine that many a group of New England farmers and old codgers sat around stoves in country stores for decades after 1816 arguing their heads off about the causes of "the year eighteen hundred and froze to death," as it became named. One can just hear them arguing. "Why Ned, I think it was them thar sun spots what did it?" "Sun spots! Listen to that thar nonsense, wouldya, boys! Gawd knows it was the moon. The moon didn't look right all summer. Could tell something was wrong."

Not only farmers argued about it; so did scientists. They fought it out in their journals. Interestingly, the scientists did no better than the average farmer in guessing the cause of the cold. For example, Ernst Chaldni of Germany wrote in *Annalen der Physik* that more icebergs than normal had broken loose in the North Atlantic and had drifted southward to cool the ocean. He developed this theory after reading in a few ship's logs that more icebergs than normal had been sighted. But the theory was wrong. First of all, the prevailing winds during that summer in North America came not from the Atlantic Ocean, but overland from the west. More importantly, a few ships' logs were not enough to provide a true picture of the iceberg situation in the North Atlantic. Furthermore, it would have taken warm weather to break the icebergs loose rather than cold weather. And last but not least, a few icebergs cannot cool down a huge ocean. Other scientific conjectures of the time were equally fantastical.

There were plenty of crackpot theories. Several writers blamed it all on Benjamin Franklin. Benjamin Franklin? What did he have to do with it? According to one theory, the hot interior of the earth releases heat into the atmosphere. But because of Franklin's newly invented lightning rods, which now were being installed all over the country, the earth's heat rise was slowed down and the air became colder. Others had a different way of seeing it. Since lightning is heat, the lightning rods had taken heat out of the air.

What is strangest in all of this is that Benjamin Franklin had hit upon the cause of odd cold spells. He had written that volcanic ash lying for months high in the atmosphere might be able to block out enough sunlight to cool down parts of the earth.

Scientists today are quite sure that a gigantic volcanic explosion in 1815 caused the cold summer following. In 1815 Mount Tambora in the Dutch East Indies literally exploded. An enormous column of smoke and ash ascended into the atmosphere.

The explosion was actually greater than that of the famous Krakatoa explosion of 1883. Geologists measuring the remains of Mount Tambora's 1815 crater say that twenty-five cubic miles of ash went into the air. This dust remained in the upper atmosphere for well over a year. As it did so, it spread outward until it was in a very, very thin layer extending for thousands of miles. Though these layers could hardly be seen from the earth, they were enough to reflect some of the sun's heat back into outer space. And that was enough to affect the temperature over a huge area of land and sea. We have seen, however, that it was not enough to cool down the whole world—far from it. As large as eastern North America, the Atlantic Ocean (where cooling no doubt took place), and western Europe are, they form only a small part of the earth's total surface area. Somehow, because of wind patterns, ash shot out of volcano in what is now Indonesia finally affected the weather in eastern North America and western Europe.

Why didn't New Englanders or Europeans know what caused the cold weather that summer? To begin with, very few even knew of the Tambora volcano. After all, the explosion was on the other side of the world in the far-off East Indies. Even had they known about it, could they have expected that the dust from the volcano would affect them? Only the later close study of many volcanic eruptions, using computer printouts of wind patterns, dust layers, and dust reflectivity, have convinced today's scientists that Tambora was the cause of the cold weather of 1816. Stephen H. Schneider and Clifford Mass of the National Center for Atmospheric Research in Boulder, Colorado, worked out the basic computer models to simulate the conditions of the summer of 1816. Some of the results of their research were presented in *Scientific American,* June 1979.

The history of that summer is grim, especially since it leaves us with a vulnerable feeling. At any time a huge volcano might explode, as Mount St. Helens recently did. Compared to Tambora that eruption was tiny, but there is no telling when a large volcano might erupt. At any time there might be enough dust blown out into the atmosphere to block out enough incoming sunlight to cool down large land areas.

By the way, a large enough asteroid exploding leaves dust in the air as well. That too could bring about a disaster. Our food crops are vulnerable. A few degrees below normal at the wrong time and they can die. Crop failures can be followed by famines. Someday in the near or distant future there will undoubtedly be another year without a summer. Will it be next year? Ten years from now? A hundred years from now? Who knows?

3. The Galveston Hurricane of 1900

More people died in the Galveston hurricane than in all the other violent storms mentioned in this book put together. Today, over eight decades later, a great deal is known about hurricanes, nature's most powerful storms.

Hurricanes begin to develop over tropical seas where water temperature is at least 82°F. They begin their life in the tropical easterlies, sometimes also called the trade winds. These winds usually blow from the east or northeast at about 30° N latitude. Actually, hurricanes will not form south of latitude 6° N.

It is during the late summer and autumn that the seas in the tropics north of the equator are at their warmest. For months they have been warming up. Yet now, at the same time, the northern hemisphere is cooling down. As the easterlies move over the warm seas, they are buffeted by cool winds coming from the north. These arrive in high-pressure areas, called anticyclones. The winds rotate in a clockwise direction. When an anticyclone is aloft and crosses the path of the easterlies it sets up disturbances in the flow of the trade winds. They appear to give the easterlies a twisting motion, which forms whirlpools of air in them. This happens rather frequently. A lot of these disturbances end up as tropical rain squalls and gusty weather and not much else.

Every now and then the whirlpool of air, moving slowly in a counterclockwise direction, will develop into a tropical depression. This means that the air in the center of the whirlpool of air (a cyclone, strictly speaking) is warm, moist, and has a low barometric pressure. The air around it is drier, cooler, and has a higher barometric pressure. The cool, dense air naturally tends to flow toward the area of the cyclone where the air is less dense. This flow of air circles inward. It also forces the lightweight warm, moist air to rise up in the center of the cyclone. When that happens, the water vapor condenses and rain starts falling.

As the water vapor condenses, the latent heat in it is released. This heat powers the storm. The temperature difference between the sea-level outer parts of a tropical depression and the center can be as much as $18°F$. In the upper atmosphere, the air is at temperatures that are below zero. The vertical air temperatures can go from $80°F$ at sea level in the storm's center to below zero in the high clouds.

Once a storm gets started, it tends to perpetuate itself. The more air and warm moisture it can pull into itself, the more powerful it will become. A large hurricane, when fully developed, is so powerful that it can move 3.5 billion tons of air per hour.

When the winds in a tropical cyclonic storm reach 74 miles per hour, the storm is considered a hurricane. It has a characteristic circular shape. A satellite photo shows it as a great round, swirling pattern of clouds. A hurricane can be as large as twelve hundred miles in diameter. Most, however, are about five hundred miles in diameter. In the middle of the storm is an eye of calm. Though the rest of the storm is cloudy, a person inside the storm's eye can see blue sky above. The eye of a hurricane can vary from about twelve to sixty miles in diameter.

The inner structure of a hurricane is interesting. Rain clouds form into distinct, well-organized bands. These are from six to twelve miles in width and from about sixty to ninety miles in length. Many of these bands spiral about the eye of the hurricane. Torrential rains fall—commonly five to ten inches during a single storm. If it were not for the high winds, the space between the bands would probably be free of rain. As it is, they are filled with veils of wind-swept rain, which comes from the bands of rain clouds. A person in a hurricane cannot determine if the rain hitting him is wind blown or is falling directly on him from the rain clouds above. In fact, it was only when meteorologists probed hurricanes with radar that the distinct rain bands were discovered.

It seems odd that the center of the storm—the eye—could be dead calm. There is an explanation. As the peripheral winds race in toward the eye, they move so fast that they set up a centrifugal force, which pushes the winds back away from the center.

One can ask, "If that is the case, where do the winds go?" They spiral swiftly upward inside the sides of the eye. The winds, carrying their loads of warm, moist air, race up the funnel-shaped eye, which is widest at the top. Some of the air reaches an elevation of about fifty thousand feet above sea level. As the air rises, the cooling effects of the air's expansion at higher altitudes condenses the moisture, and more rain falls.

Hurricane winds always stir up the sea, producing huge waves. It is not at all uncommon for hurricane waves to be thirty feet high. Some twice as high have been seen. These waves are much more destructive than the winds.

The high winds and low-pressure area near the center of the

storm produce a hurricane tide. This tide has nothing to do with the usual tides, which are produced by the pull of the sun and (especially) the moon on the seas. The word *tide* is unfortunate, for people confuse the two phenomena. A hurricane tide can easily rise six or seven feet and, under very unusual circumstances, can be as high as twenty feet. This tide can be accompanied by high waves, which add to its height and power. Occasionally, a hurricane tide arrives with the normal lunar high tide, making the storm even more destructive.

Hurricanes have a life-span of from a few hours to several weeks. The average life-span is from five to ten days.

The paths that hurricanes take are so varied and at times so unusual that it is impossible to describe an average path. Most move along with the easterlies during their infancies. As they grow stronger, they most often head north. In the later part of their lives they move more toward the north-northeast. Such a path will look like a letter C. Some hurricanes' paths are very long, going from the ocean region near the Cape Verde Islands to Cuba and then northward as far as Newfoundland.

Once a hurricane crosses over the land, it starts dying. It lacks the needed warm, moist air that only the open sea provides in large enough quantity. Once inland, the force of the hurricane's winds will die down within hours. Hurricane damage is rarely experienced more than one hundred miles from the sea. Also the farther north a hurricane goes over the ocean, the cooler the water will be. Lacking the necessary heat, the hurricane's winds will die down. It will end its life as just another storm over the North Atlantic.

It should be noted that several other storms, namely typhoons, the so-called cyclones of the Indian Ocean, and the Willy-Willies of Australia are all hurricanes. The only difference between one in the northern hemisphere and the southern hemisphere is that the wind directions change. In the southern hemisphere, all hurricanes revolve in a clockwise direction, rather than in a counterclockwise direction, as they do in the north.

At the turn of the century, Galveston, Texas, was a major deepwater port. Sailing ships, steamers, and freighters docked at its wharves. The city was bustling, wealthy, proud. Thirty-eight thousand people lived there. Thousands lived in shanties near the docks. Lining the beaches stood the substantial homes of the middle classes, who were mostly merchants. Along beautiful boulevards decorated with palms and oleanders were the ornate mansions of the rich. There were large churches, an orphanage, a convent, hospitals, new apartment buildings, and an army fort and other public buildings. It was an up-and-coming city. Many said it was destined to be the most important in the South.

On the afternoon of September 7, 1900, very few in Galveston imagined that in twenty-four hours the city would be destroyed. One of America's worst storm disasters would befall the city. In terms of deaths, there has been nothing like it before or since.

A few members of the staff of the Weather Bureau had an inkling that a storm was brewing. Sailors visiting the local houses of ill repute told women there that their ships had come through "sheer hell." Someplace out there was a storm of gigantic proportions. The meteorologists at the Weather Bureau had already received cables informing them that a hurricane had devastated Trinidad. They knew that it was wandering around, either someplace in the Gulf of Mexico or the Caribbean Sea. But where? In those days, before the time of airplane patrols, radar, and satellites, it was impossible to follow a storm. Hurricanes moved faster than the information about them. Then the men at the Weather Bureau saw the barometer fall, the wind speed change, the humidity go up. They also noted a change in the sea waves beating on the Galveston beaches.

Acting on information given by the Weather Bureau, the local newspaper published a forecast for the next day: hurricane. There it was in black and white. Anyone who took heed of the notice and left had no problems and was sure of survival. Regrettably, almost everyone ignored the warning. Only a handful of people left the island on which Galveston was located. In fact, many took excursion trains *to* the city. On September 8, large numbers of sightseers arrived. One of the attractions for them was the raging surf.

People flocked into Galveston in spite of the fact that hurricane flags were whipping in the stiff breeze. They were oblivious to any sense of danger. Though most knew that the highest spot of the island was a little less than nine feet above sea level, they nevertheless came to see the big waves, which were already close to twenty feet high! Isaac Cline, an employee of the Weather Bureau, took a horse and sulky and rode up and down the beach and waterfront to tell people to leave, that a hurricane was on its way and they were in mortal danger. Many, sitting on blankets and eating picnic lunches, stared at him as though he were insane. Others laughed. A few called him a prophet of doom and told him to run off and stop being such a killjoy.

There was, according to one witness, the most beautiful sky he had ever seen. He likened the clouds to fish scales. Each scale glowed with subdued nacreous, rainbow colors.

The breeze increased in force. The hurricane flags were getting ripped as they snapped in the wind. People thrilled to the sight of the enormous waves that arced up out of the sea and fell on the beach sand with a thunderous roar. A few daring souls splashed about in the surf. It was a scene of terrible irony. Many who frolicked there would soon be dead.

One of the regular beach attractions was the Pagoda, a structure shaped like an oriental pagoda and covering about two blocks. To the amazement of the crowd, waves demolished it in front of their eyes seemingly without effort. The great building sank into the water and in minutes became a disordered mass of floating timbers. Many people seeing that finally realized that perhaps the storm they were watching so happily might be larger and more powerful than they had thought it to be. Groups slowly drifted away from the beaches and went home.

Meteorologists watched the barometer fall. It hit 28.5 inches and kept on falling. The winds rose. By early afternoon they hit hurricane force. Howling winds swept the island. Water rose onto the beaches. Tourists realized that they were in for more excitement than they had ever bargained for. Things began to fly through the air: papers, lawn furniture, tree limbs. People ran. Telephone poles and wires fell down, hitting some pedestrians. Then a terrible thing happened. The city, in years past plagued by fires, had ordered that all downtown buildings have their roofs covered with tiles as a protection against flying sparks from any fire. The hurricane-force winds ripped away tens of thousands of tiles from the roofs. They went whizzing through the air, cutting people down. Horrified onlookers saw pedestrians decapitated by the tiles. To be on the streets was to face the possibility of instant death.

The waves grew larger and larger. The tide went up and water swept into the city. At first it lapped over the wharves, then it flooded shanties, harborside bars, warehouses. Thousands of poor people lived by the water. Their houses were no longer a safe refuge. Their only hope was to run for it to the richer sections of town, farther inland. But their route was blocked by the hail of flying tiles. The choice was between risking two forms of death.

A great number of poor people made it to the solid granite homes of the rich, which were located away from the water. Although this was sixty years before the first civil-rights marches, the wealthy took in without exception every single person who asked for shelter. Black laborers, Chinese sailors, whores, gamblers, and poor of all descriptions and races were given immediate shelter. There was not one report that anyone had been turned down.

The wealthy offered the refugees tea and cookies. As the storm howled outside and windows began to break and the houses shake, rich and poor sang hymns together and held long prayer meetings. Outside they could hear the cries of the injured and dying.

As the afternoon hours passed, the force of the hurricane increased. Gigantic waves ripped away wharves and set ships loose. Waters crept into houses. The first floors became flooded. The waters continued to rise. Building foundations were loosened. Within a few short hours, the first floors of most houses were deep under water. Families had to take refuge in upstairs rooms.

The power of a wave is almost beyond belief. Each cubic yard of water weighs a little under a ton. A wave 10 feet high and 30 feet long pushing against a house would have about 90 tons of force. Imagine then the power of such a wave slamming against the walls of a house. In addition to that is the pressure of the wind— a hurricane wind of 75 miles per hour exerts a force of about 100 pounds per square foot. With such forces pushing against them, houses began to tumble over. Others were battered to pieces by floating timbers, railroad ties, and loosened ships.

People who survived the destruction of their homes, clung for dear life to roofs, to floating beams. Those who lived saw about them a terrible scene. Waves washed people off roofs; tossing beams knocked children out of the grip of parents. Swimmers gave up and sank beneath the waves. The air was filled with flying debris, the howling noises of the winds, and the terrified screams of the dying.

Anna Delz's experience was one of the more dramatic. In the afternoon her mother and sister had gone out, leaving her at home. Sixteen-year-old Anna had a friend visiting her. They were alone in the house. As the hurricane progressed, they saw water creep onto the first floor. Anna and her girl friend packed valuables in a trunk and lugged it upstairs to the second floor. There they waited for the winds to die down. But instead of dying down, the winds increased in speed. Soon waves were pounding the side of the house and getting into the second-floor rooms. The girls watched the water rise into those rooms. The walls shook. Anna heard a loud crash as the house collapsed around them. She never saw her friend again. Stunned, floating in the water, and driven along by the wind, Anna came to a standing tree and managed to climb into it. Then she saw a detached rooftop with twenty women and children on it. Anna figured it would be a safer place to be than the tree. Also there would be company. She swam to the roof and got on it with the others.

The loose-floating roof plowed through the raging waters. Waves rocked it precariously. Spray blown by winds traveling over 100 miles per hour blinded them. Boards and timbers thrown over the roof by the waves knocked people into the water, usually killing them outright. Others were cut down by flying tiles. Before long Anna saw that she was alone on the roof. She also knew she could not stay on it much longer, for tossing boards were battering it to pieces.

When the roof finally came apart, Anna swam into the swirling waters and grabbed a large solid timber. With great difficulty she climbed on it. All around her were unforgettable scenes of disaster and horror. Dozens of people near her clung to wood, branches, railroad ties, and broken porch columns. Time and again she saw people slip away and drown. Countless corpses bobbed up and down on the waves, many brushing against her. Over and over again she saw sturdy-looking houses collapse before the onslaught of the hurricane.

The Galveston, Texas, hurricane of 1900 left the city in ruins. Many bodies were buried in the piles of wreckage. *National Archives*

After a while, she realized to her horror that the waves were carrying her away from the city and out to sea. The tide was changing and resultant currents pulled her ever farther out. She soon found herself alone in the Gulf of Mexico. Time and again she struggled to stay on the rolling timber as it pitched, rolled, and bucked over titanic waves. By all accounts, the waves were probably sixty feet high. Her timber rode up on them as high as a six-story building, only to plummet down again. As she struggled, pieces of her clothing were ripped off until she had nothing on. Thirsty, hungry, tired, naked, and utterly alone on the sea, she continued to fight for her life. She was certain that

each wave was taking her farther and farther from land. Some people would have surrendered themselves to the waves. But not Anna.

Fortunately, the wind was steadily blowing toward the land, and the tidal currents again changed. So, unknown to Anna, the timber she was on was now pitching and rolling through the darkness toward land. It entered the bay between Galveston Island and the Texas coast, finally coming to the railroad bridge, by then a bent and broken maze of iron. Anna was so exhausted that she decided to abandon the timber and hold on to the bridge to gain her strength. The darkness luckily hid a

terrible sight from her eyes. After the hurricane, forty-eight
naked bodies were found caught in the steel maze of the bridge.

After hanging onto the bridge awhile, the cold numbed her
too much. The wind blowing on her wet body made her shiver.
Anna decided she had to get back into the water, which was
actually quite warm. She swam to the next piece of driftwood
that came by. The wood carried her all the way across Galveston Bay to the Texas mainland. Her driftwood raft was driven
by the wind into an enormous pile of wood. Anna carefully
climbed onto the huge stack. Feeling her way along so as not to
get cut, she finally reached the top of the pile. The wind at last
was dying down. She realized that the woodpile was stable and
would not be moved either by the waves or the wind. Utterly
exhausted she lay down and went to sleep. When she woke up
she was warm and dry, for the Texas sun was shining on her.
Though stark naked and bruised, she was alive.

Most people who survived the waves usually did so on roofs,
clinging to timbers, and through other such means, but others
used more unusual methods. One man rode out the storm in a
large barrel. Seeing that he could not escape the waves, he got
inside a handy barrel and was able to secure the cover of it so
that the inside was watertight. All night he bounced up and
down on the waves. Inside he could hear the wind, feel objects
hitting his barrel, hear the screams of drowning people. Only
when he was positive that he was perfectly safe did he open the
cover and look around.

Another man was forced into the upper floor of a house.
There he found two very large glass bottles. He tied himself to
them, so that one would be on each side of his body. Carefully,
so as not to break either bottle, he got into the water. All night
he had to fend off solid objects that could have smashed a bottle.
Somehow he managed it, and he too lived.

Some tried to survive by tying themselves in trees. This usually did not work. In some cases the water rose right over the

treed people, drowning them. Others in trees were helplessly cut to ribbons by flying objects. But some did survive that way. The family of the Reverend L. P. Davis found themselves trapped by the water and waves. They figured their last hope was to climb into some tall trees near their house and tie themselves to the tree trunks, so they did. All night the hurricane winds swayed the trees. Limbs cracked off. Fortunately the people were in a rather isolated location, so they were not cut down by flying glass, tiles, or boards. Most of their clothes, however, were ripped off of them. When the waters went down, wind-driven sand almost flayed their skin. So much salt water was unavoidably swallowed that they were sick. After cutting the ropes, the family members dropped down on the sand, too weary to move. Reverend Davis walked for help. He was only barely able to make it to a distant house. The owner of the house gave him a horse and wagon with which he could pick up and move his family. That was not good enough. The family was too weak to travel. And then a steer almost as exhausted as they were came by. They fell upon it, butchering it and drinking the blood.

After the sea and wind had destroyed almost all the shanties, seaside saloons, and wooden frame houses, it attacked the stronger structures. The city had many sturdy buildings built of granite or bricks: orphanages, churches, mansions, apartment buildings, convents. It also had lighthouses and even a coastal artillery fort. No one would have dreamed that any of these structures would crumble in the face of a hurricane.

One structure that offered refuge from the storm was Bolivar Lighthouse. When people realized the power of the storm, many raced to take shelter there. Quite a few who went there came from a train that was stranded. A virtual mob crowded into the lighthouse in a state of panic. Soon it was packed. It was so crowded that people sat in the laps of strangers, mostly on the steps of the spiraling staircase inside the heavy stone walls. After the last person got in, the heavy door at the foot of the stairs was closed. Waters quickly rose around the base of the lighthouse. The people packed into the upper stairwell. The door was soon deep under water. High winds hitting over 120 miles per hour buffeted the structure. It was pitch black inside, and in the darkness people heard frightening sounds: screaming winds, heavy objects slamming into the lighthouse, the roar and thunder of heavy waves and surf. The air soon became fetid. Sitting in cramped positions for hours, many suffered from muscular pains.

The situation was literally maddening. People sobbed, screamed, or became angered by their pain. Since there was no drinking water, thirst tormented them. Unable to move, with no sanitary facilities, the stairwell soon oozed with human excreta. Some, smelling it, vomited. They were almost suffocated by the bad odor, but they were trapped. The only escape route was through the door, which was at least thirty feet under water. Many wished they were dead. However, none died. When the waters receded so that they could get to the door and escape, they ran out into the sunlight. But they only ran a few feet before they stopped to stand silently together. All around the base of the lighthouse lay a mass of dead bodies. The survivors were shocked. Now some felt shame for their hysteria and rage. Suddenly thankful to be among the living, they sank to their knees and thanked God for saving them.

Fifty people took refuge in the Cline Home, a solid masonry structure that could supposedly withstand any hurricane. Those inside the Home heard the sea slamming the walls. The building shook, but it was more than holding its own. The thick walls could hold back the strongest wave. Then a new noise sounded in the darkness, a great pounding noise. The enormous waves were battering the walls with a two-hundred-pound section of railroad bridge. A steel rail protruded from it. The bridge section hit the walls with one wave, got pulled far back with the next, and then came hurtling against the walls with the next.

Again and again this happened until finally the walls cracked and began to come down. And then the whole building went at once. People who were not crushed outright went tumbling into the waves. All perished.

At the large St. Mary's Cathedral, priests who had tried to find shelter from the storm there realized that the whole structure was about to fall down. They gave each other the last rites. Just as they finished, the church tower fell. A huge metal bell ripped from the tower fell down through the air, clanging loudly. In minutes the church was a rubble heap. No one knows how many died in the cathedral.

At the Lucas Flats, a brick apartment building then considered extraordinarily up-to-date, a terrifyingly deadly game was being played. One by one the apartments crumbled in the wind. Walls crashed down. Ceilings collapsed, burying people under them. The game the people played was like musical chairs. As apartment after apartment went, they had to guess which of those remaining were safe. Everyone there raced back and forth from one apartment to another. Those who guessed right lived a little longer, until that apartment too went. In the end only one apartment remained intact. Jonathan Hale and Mary Quayle, who had just seen her husband die, were in it. Of the nearly one hundred people who lived at Lucas Flats, only twenty survived, most of them by being someplace else that night.

The Ursuline Convent was a large stone-and-brick structure covering four city blocks. Around the convent was a ten-foot-high brick wall. For much of the storm the buildings of the convent were protected by the wall. For hours the waves threw themselves at the wall. Spray driven by hurricane winds flew over the top of the wall. Heavy debris battered the wall. For hours the wall held, but nothing could hold out against the hurricane indefinitely and finally the wall crumbled. Water rushed through as it would through a broken dam. The nuns in the convent saw the waves roll in with a cargo of boxcars, trees, corpses, rooftops. In all that mess were living humans: men, women, and children. The nuns immediately went to work to rescue them. Leaning from windows and using poles they dragged people inside.

One person they rescued was Mrs. William Henry Heideman, who was about to have a baby. She was all alone. Earlier that evening she had clung to a roof. The winds had taken her on a terrible ride all through Galveston, past flooded homes, collapsing buildings, floating corpses, and broken railroad boxcars. Helter skelter she went, seeing more horror in a few hours than most people see in a lifetime. She might have given up but for the baby inside of her. When the roof she was on began to come apart, it seemed the end must be near for her. Just then a very large steamer trunk floated near her. It was empty. Though she was pregnant, somehow she managed to get into it. It carried her away, bobbing up and down over the raging waves, eventually floating her to the convent. The nuns pulled her in through a window. They took her to a nun's cell where she immediately gave birth to a boy.

By odd coincidence her brother-in-law floated to the convent at about the same time, although it was a long way from his house. He had managed to grab a tree limb and pull himself to a standing tree. Just as he got settled there he saw a young boy floundering in the water below, swiftly being carried off by the current. He got out of the tree, rescued the boy, and with great difficulty pulled him up into the branches. When he had a chance to see whom he had just rescued, he was amazed. It was his nephew! A little while later the nuns were able to get them into the convent.

Another man rescued by the nuns was Mr. James Irwin, whose house had collapsed. He swam through the waves, trying to find something to hold on to, when he was swept up to the convent. The nuns pulled him through a window. They were

momentarily stunned, for he was naked. Then one nun ran and
got a habit that had been worn by an exceptionally large nun.
Irwin put it on it. It fit. Now dressed as a nun, he immediately
went to work giving first aid to people. A few dazed people were
puzzled at the bearded nun helping them. One hurricane victim
was even more astounded. It was his wife, who had thought he
was dead.

Protected during the worst phase of the hurricane by the wall
surrounding it, the Ursuline convent, though heavily damaged,
survived. So did those lucky enough to have been rescued by the
nuns. So did the eight babies delivered there that night.

Not too far away, the Old Women's Home caved in. Though
people knew it was in danger, no one could get to it. The water
was too deep, the currents too swift, the waves too high. From
a distance, people saw it go. None of the people in the home
were seen alive again.

Far down the beach, heavy ten-inch coastal defense guns protected the harbor and bay. The guns were in concrete emplacements built to withstand an enemy bombardment. To get into
them one had to open steel doors weighing hundreds of pounds.
The doors faced away from the sea.

When the storm arrived it wiped out the barracks where the
troops were stationed. All the soldiers were lost in the storm.
The commanding officer, Captain W. C. Rafferty, decided at
almost the last moment that he and his family would be safe if
they could get into a gun emplacement. His family and maid
followed him through the howling winds to an emplacement.
With difficulty Captain Rafferty opened the huge door. They
all got down inside and shut the door. Crouched together in the
small cramped quarters, they listened to the storm. The wind
and waves were so powerful they ripped away ten-inch cannons
and broke down gun emplacements. In the night, above the din
of the storm, they could hear the rumble of cannons rolling
about near them. At one point the wind pried open the steel

door. The maid went popping out into the storm. Though the captain took a flying leap to catch her, he missed. She was never seen again. He then turned his attention to the door. If it remained open, they would all die, for they would be flooded out or sucked away by the wind. Exerting utmost effort, he struggled until he got the door closed. He and his family just barely survived the storm.

What damage the wind and waves could not do, loose ships were doing. Runaway ships of all types, sizes, and descriptions were adrift, battering down buildings, docks, and bridges. Along with the wind and high seas, they demolished all the bridges connecting Galveston with mainland Texas. Several ships were blown over thirty miles that night. Most of those that hit rocks sank immediately, with a heavy loss of life among the crews. Sailors on one ship, however, heard the vessel bouncing for hours on boulders. They knew that any second the seams could split open and water pour in on them. It never happened. Though the sailors were banged around and bruised, the ship's hull remained intact. Other ships were pushed miles inland, so that when the storm ended, they were sitting in the middle of Galveston or in some farmer's field.

All storms, no matter how terrible, must end, and so did the great Galveston hurricane. After midnight, the winds let up a bit. By dawn they had lessened considerably. When the sun rose there was only a stiff breeze.

The survivors that morning witnessed one of the most devastating scenes ever seen in America. Half of all the buildings in Galveston were completely destroyed. Almost no house or building escaped heavy damage. What remained was in a chaotic state almost beyond imagining. Amid ruined, smashed houses lay the pilings of broken bridges, smashed boxcars, ships, telephone poles and wires, dead horses, dead pigs, and the corpses of thousands of people.

Even after the hurricane the survivors had to fight for their lives. There was no electricity, no water, no food, no medical supplies. In addition they were isolated and could not get to the mainland for help. The bridges were ruined, and mangled, drowned bodies laced the steel. No one could leave the island by ship, as not one ship or boat was to be had. In short, the survivors were marooned on an island of death.

The rest of the world knew that something terrible had happened in Galveston. Since the afternoon before, when the hurricane had just started to get rolling, knocking down telephone and telegraph wires, no one had been able to reach Galveston. Texans, seeing the mainland coast get hit by the fierce winds, knew that Galveston was getting it much worse. By night some Texans were sure that everyone in Galveston must be dead. Even the staid *New York Times* was so sure by late evening that the city must be gone that the paper printed headlines stating

Few buildings, even those built of stone, escaped damage during the Galveston hurricane. *National Archives*

Galveston had been demolished. Unknown to people in Galveston, help was on its way almost before the hurricane blew itself out.

On the island, Galvestonians knew they had to do something fast. But what? Since most of the elected officials were dead, ad hoc governmental committees were formed. To increase the police force, able-bodied men were deputized. But what was most important? Water? Electricity? Hospitalization of the wounded? Obtaining medical supplies? Burial of the dead, who were already rotting in the hot sun? Protection against looters? Rescue of trapped people? Each difficulty was handled as well as possible. The people of Galveston began emergency work right away.

Soon ships, boats, and even rafts carrying emergency supplies were coming from the mainland to Galveston. A railroad bridge was repaired. But along with help came hordes of curiosity seekers and looters. Army units patrolled the streets and often shot looters. Some looters were found with pocketfuls of fingers and ears, quickly cut off so they could get rings and earrings. More upsetting to the Galvestonians were men who photographed dead, naked women. There were reports that some of the photographers were shot. This probably never happened, although many people would gladly have shot them.

For a couple of days there was a terrible water shortage. Rescue workers feared many people more would die of thirst. A massive effort was mounted to bring barrels of drinking water to the city.

The next most pressing problem was disposal of the dead. They were literally everywhere. One could hardly walk a block without seeing corpses. A terrible stench filled the air. Doctors coming into the city feared that diseases would quickly spread among the living. As time wore on, the air became almost unbreathable because of the putrid odors. Almost everyone wore cotton gauze over their mouth and nose. Those who could get camphor balls tied them onto the gauze masks to help cut the odor.

Though thousands of people wanted to identify their dead relatives and friends, officials decided to take the corpses to sea and immediately dump them. Drafted crews, forced into labor often at gunpoint, picked up corpses and loaded them on barges. It was an offense even to take a ring off of a finger. One worker started to take a large diamond ring off the finger of a dead woman but was threatened with death if he did so. He sorrowfully shrugged his shoulders and hoisted the dead woman into a barge.

The charnal barges were towed to sea, and the corpses dumped into the water. Unfortunately, the corpses floated and the wind blew them right back to Galveston. Officials, by now genuinely terrified by the growing public health problems, declared that the corpses had to be burned. Huge piles of broken boards, easily obtainable, were put together, and the corpses laid on them. Crowds of sobbing, screaming people who wanted a chance to see their loved ones for the last time, if at all possible, had to be held back as torches lit crudely improvised crematory fires. Saddened army troops restrained mothers, fathers, and children. The huge pyres burned and smoke filled the air. One pyre alone held over one thousand corpses. A thick, stomach-turning smoke, reeking of burning, rotting flesh hung over Galveston. And then a few days later, the air was clear again. The dead were gone; the air smelled clean and of the sea. Galveston had been saved from what could have been a terrible epidemic.

The people of Galveston were absolutely determined to rebuild. Since most of the city officials were dead, the most prominent men got together and established a city council to govern the city— the first city council in American history. It worked so well and so effectively that other cities began to adopt it as a form of government. The council form now has a permanent place in our urban legal system.

After the count was taken, it was realized that as many as eight thousand people had died in the terrible hurricane. This is by far the largest toll of violent death suffered in any American disaster from any cause whatsoever. Nothing comparable has ever happened in the United States.

4. The New England Hurricane of 1938

Those of us who were in the 1938 hurricane remember how it took us by surprise. Like the bombing of Pearl Harbor, it was totally unexpected.

It was known that hurricanes had ravaged New England in the dim past. But most meteorologists doubted that those so-called hurricanes actually were tropical hurricanes, that is to say, swirling masses of air that had developed over tropical seas and traveled northward. They were quite sure that the storms mentioned had been local disturbances that had acted very much like tropical hurricanes. Of course, there was no way of proving what the case was. In the seventeenth, eighteenth, and nineteenth centuries, record keeping was too primitive to track that kind of storm.

In most ways, the 1938 New England hurricane was a typical hurricane. In other ways it was aberrant. Most distinctive was the way it snuck up on the United States' Northeast.

In mid-September, ships—one was the *Alegrete* of Brazil—

reported high winds five hundred miles northeast of the Lee-
ward Islands. A lot of ships reported them. The winds were not
hurricane force, however. While the storm zigzagged about,
hundreds of miles off the North American coast, meteorologists
receiving radio reports decided that there was not much to
worry about. Sailors on the reporting ships agreed. By the twentieth of September the storm was still not a full-fledged hurricane.

Then a very unusual thing happened. The rotating storm
started northward, heading directly for Long Island, New York.
At 8:30 P.M., September 20, the storm system was far off the
Florida coast. By 8:30 A.M., September 21, it was off Cape Hat-
teras. And then the whole storm system shot north at record-
breaking speeds. By 3:30 P.M. it was slamming into the Long
Island shore and threatening nearby New England. It had bar-
reled northward, covering five hundred miles in a mere seven
hours! Its average speed was 73 miles per hour, the fastest sprint
made by any hurricane ever recorded. No wonder it occasioned
such surprise.

Before the hurricane hit, September 21 was a calm day,
warmer than normal for that time of year. All along the coast,
people were trying to get in their last swim of the season or lying
in the sun burnishing their suntan. Children were getting used
to the idea of being in school again. A perfect day. Who would
have ever guessed it was a perfect day for a hurricane?

By the time radio announcers in New York City reported
that a hurricane was imminent, rains from the hurricane had
already flooded sections of the city subway system. Many trains
were not running; hundreds of thousands of commuters were
stranded. High winds swept over the tall skyscrapers. The
Empire State Building swayed sixteen inches back and forth in
the wind. Torrents of rain stopped traffic. A few people caught
in their cars by flash floods and unable to get to safety drowned.
In the parks and suburbs trees fell. Broken live electrical wires

writhed like snakes on the ground, with sparks that hissed and crackled.

But New York City was not in the eye of the hurricane. It was only sideswiped.

Things were much, much worse on Long Island. At about 3:30 P.M. the full force of the storm plowed into the island. Then it moved on New England.

I was living in New England at the time—in Rockport, Massachusetts—and my experience was typical of that of millions of others that day.

I recall the day very well. Like just about everyone else in town, I was surprised that it was so warm and so calm that day. I went to school without a jacket or sweater. At recess we boys played baseball. It was so warm that we took off our shirts. That was almost unheard of so late in the season. After all, September 21 is the first day of autumn. It was a true Indian summer, better than any I could previously remember.

I left school at 3:30 P.M. and played with some friends. After an hour, I got on my bike and rode to the Curtiss Newsstand to pick up the afternoon newspapers for my paper route. When I got there, I noticed that everyone in the room was huddled around the radio. A man's voice speaking through the static was saying something about gigantic waves and floods in Providence, Rhode Island. He said that most of the city had been swept away. According to him, Providence had virtually been wiped out!

I could not understand. Wiped out? How? Waves? Floods? What waves? What floods? It did not make any sense. I asked. I was told to be quiet. I waited and asked again.

"It's a hurricane," said an old man. "It's a hurricane and it's coming this way."

"Go home," said Mr. Curtiss. "You won't be delivering any papers today."

"They'll all blow away," said another.

They listened some more. I huddled close and heard of bridges down, trains swamped, towns wiped out. I felt frightened and excited all at once. One part of me was saying, "This is terrible. Maybe I'll die." Another part of me was saying, "Hey, this is exciting. It's about time something happened around here."

Mr. Curtiss turned to me and said, "Go on home, Junior. Your father wants you to help him."

That surprised me. Help him do what? I wondered. "What's he want me for?" I asked.

"You are going to get in trouble with your old man if you don't get moving," said another man.

I ran out of the newsstand and got on my bike. As I sped down Main Street, my head was filled with a dozen thoughts. A hurricane? Gee. It sure didn't look like it. It's so calm. Providence wiped out? Then it occurred to me that if there were a hurricane coming there might be large waves on the ocean. Rockport was right on the sea. I pedaled my bike to a small park at the end of Bear Skin Neck, a point of land jutting out into the ocean. From there I got an unobstructed view of the sea.

What I saw will stay in my mind forever. Whenever before I had looked at the horizon it had been a straight line, indicating the relative flatness of the sea over any distance. Not that day. Gigantic waves moved along the horizon like the teeth of some titanic chain saw. There was something stately and noble about the way they moved, a strange beauty. I got off my bike and sat on the breakwater to watch. There was not a breath of wind. It was unreal for such waves to be moving along out there on such a calm day. I sat there for a long time, utterly fascinated by the sight of those marvelous waves.

Finally I recalled that my father needed me. I pulled myself away and got onto my bike. Before long I swooped into the yard, pedaling like mad. My mother and two sisters, Jeanne and Jacky, were in the yard picking pears.

"There's a hurricane. A hurricane," I yelled dramatically.

"We know it," said one of them.

"Your father's been wondering where you were," said my mother. "Now go help him. He's in the back."

I went to the back of the house. My father had just finished closing the shutters to the windows. That surprised me. Like most New England houses, our windows had shutters. But they were almost always used for decoration. Very rarely, if ever, had I seen them closed. That was interesting to me. I helped him close the rest of the shutters. Some windows did not have shutters, so we boarded them up. As we did so, I asked him dozens of questions about hurricanes. He told me all he knew about them.

After fixing the windows, my father looked at our row of poplar trees. He decided we should saw them in half. He was afraid the winds would knock them over onto the house. I hated doing it, but we sawed them all in half.

After that we joined my mother and sisters collecting fruit. We had a goodly number of apple and pear trees, and we tried to save as much ripe fruit as possible. As we were picking the apples and pears, the sky changed to a rich greenish yellow. The green appeared murky, and the yellow transparent. All seemed glazed over with a very light and delicate golden red. My father, an artist, was quite taken with the color. For the rest of his life he would occasionally refer to the layers of color in this unique and strangely tinted sky.

As interesting as the colors were the sounds in the air. Though it was still calm, we could hear a weird hollow noise coming from some indefinable, distant place. Deep and steady and musical, but also eerie and impossible to locate, the sound was frightening. Haunting and disorienting, it seemed to be everywhere and no place in particular. For all I knew, the sound could have been coming from the earth or myself or the sky. As time went on, the sound grew louder, more hollow, carrying greater reverberations.

Though it was calm on the ground, gusts of wind swept high over the house. Black scud clouds, looking like torn rags, flew overhead. Slowly the wind chopped lower. The tops of the trees began to shake.

The thought of a hurricane wind hitting our treetops excited me. I climbed to the top of an apple tree to be in it, too, and saluted the wind. I was ten years old, and I felt tremendously pleased. I knew I was in a great hurricane. I breathed in the air. It smelled of something musty. The wind felt warm and oddly pleasant against my skin. For a long time I stayed in the apple tree as it swayed back and forth. I could hear the great sound grow in volume. And then with the growing wind came the rain, sheets of it forcing me out of the tree.

Objects of various descriptions started whizzing through the air—countless leaves, twigs, pieces of paper, and the like. It was amazing how swiftly the force of the wind increased. Every gust seemed stronger than the one before.

While we ate supper, we listened to the radio. There were reports coming in of disasters everywhere. Ships had sunk, ferries had disappeared, bridges were down, houses swept out to sea.

The wind rose. It moaned and howled against the gables. The shingles were pelted with twigs, chestnuts, and the neighbors' garbage. The house, built about 1740, began to creak and every now and then it seemed to shift. It was in for its worst night in almost two hundred years of existence.

After supper my father, who was always game for anything, wanted to go to the Coast Guard station and take a look at the storm. Of course, we should never have gone, but we did. My father and I got into his heavy Packard, which looked like a gangster's car, and we drove out there. Near the Coast Guard station stood a large hotel. Some guests were outside, watching the gigantic waves and probably wondering if they should leave. The waves were like huge, rolling hills. To my amazement they swept completely over a small island opposite the Coast Guard station. On the island was a small lighthouse, which the waves easily engulfed. When they withdrew, the light would still be shining. Unfortunately, the wind was so strong and the spray so thick that one could not really get a good look at the sea. Much of what I wanted to see was lost in the spray.

When I got out of the car, I was promptly blown away. For a second I was frightened. Mostly, though, I was astonished. In spite of seeing the waves and hearing the wind, I had no idea it was that strong. I was blown into a hedge. My father had just gotten out of the car and was hanging onto the hood. I looked at him and smiled, as if to say, "Gee, this is pretty funny, isn't it?" He did not smile back, and I realized he was concerned about me. Beyond that hedge were the sea and the wild waves. It was dawning on him that our little trip to the Coast Guard station was not the most brilliant of ideas. He motioned to me to stay down. The hedge ran directly to the porch railings of the station. I crawled along the hedge to the railings.

For some reason, my father was able to stay on his feet in the wind. He came up to me, and we went into the station. Some people from the hotel were there seeking advice. From the back room I could hear coded messages arriving and being sent. On the wall was a wind-speed indicator. When gusts hit, the large needle would jump. It indicated the wind speed as 120 miles per hour at times. I stared at the needle, watching it move up and down.

A coast guardsman politely asked my father to leave. It was not a time to be bothered by curiosity seekers. We left.

I crawled on the ground to the car. Pebbles flying in the wind peppered me. It was the first time in my life I had seen a wind blowing so hard that it could pick up pebbles. We got into the car with difficulty but found we could not shut the doors against the wind. My father started up the motor and turned the car slowly around in the wide parking lot. The doors slammed shut as the wind caught them.

We drove along a little beach. My father thought that there we'd be able to see the waves. But the rain was much too heavy. In the dusk, through the swipes of the windshield wipers, I could see only a fuzzy, foggy image of rain, white foam, and spray. Luckily, we were able to make out that the road ahead was gone, washed away by the waves. We turned back up a country road that led toward our house. It took us by some fields bordered by tall trees. As we drove along the road, trees began to fall. A large one crashed in front of us, blocking our way.

Seeing it falling, my father stopped the car. For a moment he did not know what to do. Then he decided to back the car down the road and return home by way of the Coast Guard station. He put his arm on the back of the seat to look out the rear window. We started to go backward. Just then a tree fell behind us. We were trapped. Tall trees above the car swayed in the wind. At any moment one of them could fall on the car. We didn't dare get out and run for it. That would have been even more dangerous. "What are we going to do?" my father said. Just then an enormous gust of wind struck. I later learned that gusts of wind up to 186 miles per hour hit Harvard University that day, and we were closer to the storm's center than was Harvard. The car rocked as the wind hit it. The tall trees above us swayed. Limbs came down all around us. Even huge ones seemed for a split second to float away in the air. The gusts of wind grew ever stronger. The car alternately sagged and rose up on its springs.

A series of even stronger gusts of wind came along. More trees fell. Then, to our astonishment, a gust of wind lifted the tree on the road in front of us and pushed it away. The road ahead was clear. My father gunned the motor, and the heavy Packard leaped forward. In a short while we were off that tree-lined road.

We drove down Mt. Pleasant Street. On the corner of Mt. Pleasant and Pleasant streets stood a big house. A moment before we got there, a very large tree fell, slicing away a whole corner of the house. We could look right into the rooms—as though they were in a doll house. The owner stood outside assessing the damage. Rain was coming down in torrents, sweeping into the open rooms. Silver moire patterns shimmered in the falling sheets of water. Near the owner, a hysterical man ran aimlessly back and forth. He flapped his arms and elbows like chicken wings. I could see a woman picking up belongings that were blowing out of the open rooms into the yard—dresses, shirts, papers, etc. My father asked if anyone was hurt. Luckily not. He asked if we could help. They said we could not, so we drove the two blocks to our house.

Our house was quite well protected. But, since it was down in the lee of the land, all sorts of rubbish was pouring down on our property. Because of the terrain, the swift wind carrying debris would suddenly hit a dead pocket. The junk in it fell like rain. We had everyone's garbage, papers, broken lawn chairs, tree limbs, and so on in our yard. My father parked the car and we ran into the house.

The wind was giving the house quite a time. All night it shuddered and groaned in a strange way. Every drawn-out groan would end in a nervous shudder. The wind would pile up against the house, pushing it, then suddenly slip around the house. Each time it did so, the house settled back in nervous shudders.

My father told my mother all about our adventures. She merely replied that the hurricane was not as bad as a good northeaster. She told of other storms that had been much worse—or so she thought. Still, she did have a point. As far as Rockport was concerned, more damage had occurred there in some winter storms of 1934–35. My father tried to argue that this hurricane was the worst storm yet. The house shook, creaked, and groaned, and the wind howled and shrieked while they had a go-around about it. My poor father must have felt frustrated beyond words. Years later, I noticed that it was my mother who most relished telling people how we had all survived the 1938 hurricane, a little ironic twist that always amused me.

I went to bed and, to my surprise, I actually went to sleep.

I woke up before dawn. The light slowly filled the sky. The wind had died down a great deal, but there was just enough force left in it to do some last-minute damage. It picked up a small tree and threw it like a spear right through a nearby chicken house. Chickens and feathers went in all directions.

After the hurricane almost everyone in town walked or drove about, on whatever roads were clear, to see the damage. No one in Rockport was killed, but several houses were seriously damaged, roads were out, and there were fallen trees everywhere. The harbor at Gloucester, three miles from Rockport, was filled with battered and sunken ships. Cleanup was rapid and efficient. Even so, I recall that during the summer of 1939 I saw numerous places in forests where there were large masses of broken, tangled trees that had fallen in the hurricane.

Like most people in New England, we had botched-up news broadcasts during the hurricane. Some damage was exaggerated. Providence, though severely damaged, was not wiped out after all. Paradoxically, we heard nothing at first about other tragic events. Communications were so bad that even the news systems could get little information about the true nature of the hurricane. From my research, I would say that it took years for the full story to be known. At any rate, we who were in the hurricane knew very little about its full scope.

There was extensive damage from the hurricane from where it hit Long Island through New England's seaboard regions.

On the south side of Long Island are the Hamptons: East

Hampton, Southampton, Hampton Bays, and so on. During the summer they were, as they still are, popular beach resorts. Because it was a warm September 21, many more people stayed in those towns than normally would at that time of the year. Early in the afternoon of the twenty-first, people were swimming in the ocean. Others were sunbathing, or sitting in summer cottages reading mystery novels. A breeze sprang up. Soon afterward, the sky darkened, and the breeze became much stronger. People began to leave the beaches. Others took in lawn furniture so it would not get blown around. Most thought it was just a squall. The speed with which the breeze turned into a full-fledged hurricane was both amazing and frightening. The time from when the first winds were felt to the reality of a full-force hurricane was less than an hour! The winds that hit the Hamptons may have reached velocities of 200 miles per hour.

There are hundreds of eye-witness accounts of the way the hurricane hit the south shore. Naturally, each tells of the rapid rise in the wind speed. They also tell of a "tidal wave." Unfortunately, the hurricane coincided with the lunar high tide, which the wind pushed far above the normal high-tide mark. On top of all of that was the "hill" of water that accompanies so many hurricanes. Many survivors on Long Island reported one gigantic wave between thirty and forty feet high. This means it was three to four stories high. Others say that there was a series of waves, one after the other, also of the same height.

It was the wave (or waves) that killed most people. It flattened houses, tore out bridges, bent railroad tracks, carried seagoing ships ashore, and swept cars, people, and animals out to sea. Waves tore apart breakwaters, tossing ten-ton stones about and opening new channels across many of the barrier islands along the south shore.

Lining the shore at the Hamptons were fine homes belonging to wealthy families. Many of these splendid houses were to fall before the fury of the hurricane. That afternoon, Countess Charles de Ferry de Fontnouvelle, wife of the French consul general in New York City, was in a Westhampton beach house. Like everyone else, when the wind started rising she thought that a mere summer squall had started up. But to her surprise, the house soon began to shake. It shook with such violence that she thought there must be an earthquake. She then discovered that the house was shaking from the force of the wind. In addition, seawater was flooding into the basement, and the very foundation of the house was being rapidly weakened. She ran next door and asked a maid and butler there to help her, but they refused. Soon after, the countess, with her baby in her arms; Miss Agnes Zeigler, the governess; and the cook abandoned the house, which was by then shuddering to pieces. Just as they left, it tumbled. The countess watched the huge house cave in and settle to the ground. The wind and waves soon tore it to pieces. In a later interview with a *New York Times* reporter, she said she had never been so scared in all her life. But she had no time to contemplate the strange, frightening grandeur of the scene. She ran on with the other women. Planks, doors, and various pieces of metal whizzed through the air, threatening death. Any one of these could have decapitated them. Boards fell out of the air all around them. The women could hardly move in the wind. Because she was wearing overalls, which caught the wind, the countess could not make much headway. She discarded her overalls and went on in underclothes.

They got into the William Ottomans' house. The Norwegian butler, Arni Benedictson, quickly took command and calmed everyone down as more people arrived. Soon there were two dozen other refugees from the storm. He calmly made plans for their escape.

With a blinking flashlight, Benedictson signaled the mainland, reporting their situation. Then, because he was not entirely sure that people on the mainland understood or had even received the message, he left the group to cross over to the mainland. That in itself was a risky venture, for he had to cross a bridge. Huge waves were weakening it.

Before long he came back to the waiting, frightened refugees. With him were three youths: Stanley Wilson and Charles and Michael Goy. Benedictson told the refugees to link arms with him and the youths. All together, with the countess holding her baby, they started for the bridge. As they got near it, the Ottoman house went. The refugees watched in awe and terror as it collapsed and broke apart. They got to the bridge. It was swaying. Waves were smashing over it. Pieces of it were breaking away. But the refugees had to attempt a crossing. They had no choice.

When they got on to the bridge, they could feel it sinking beneath them. The air was filled with flying objects. A piece of glass sliced open Benedictson's chin and blood spurted out. Everyone felt they had only minutes left to live.

Benedictson never wavered in his efforts to get everyone across the bridge. Already the foundations of the bridge were almost gone. It hung at a slant. Huge waves, such as none any of them had ever seen, loomed up in the water and rolled toward them. The group, each helping the other, staggered forward. Just as they reached the mainland, the bridge collapsed. The countess, finally safe, looked into her baby's eyes. Later she said, "I am convinced we were spared because of the baby. Providence looked down upon us through her eyes."

Not everyone was so lucky. Not far away there was a bar filled with teenagers. One might have thought that they were all just "hanging out," but they were not. Almost every teenager in the bar had just lost one or both parents. Dazed, puzzled, they had nowhere to turn.

By the end of the day, forty-five people had been killed by the hurricane in Westhampton.

Other dramas took place on Long Island and Long Island Sound that day. Within hours the normally choppy Sound had turned into a hurricane-torn sea with gigantic waves higher than any ever seen there.

One group of people had unknowingly headed into the very heart of danger. These were the crew and passengers of the Orient Point, New York, ferryboat *The Catskill*. At 1:00 P.M. it left Orient Point for a routine crossing of the Sound to New London, Connecticut. It was a beautiful day. Passengers adjusted seats on the deck and looked forward to a pleasant ride. The water was blue, and sea gulls dipped and swayed overhead. Captain Clarence Sherman noted that the wind was up a bit. Here and there white caps appeared, seeming to wink on and off in the bright autumn sunlight. The Sound was a bit rough. Nothing unusual. Normal, really.

The ferry pushed out into the Sound. Some passengers gathered at the bow rails to watch the spray. Others at the stern watched the white wake vee its way across the waters. The flags snapped cheerfully in the brisk breeze. Most of the people were feeling sorry that summer had ended.

Minute by minute the breeze rose in force. Women had trouble with their large sun hats. Bow spray flew up over the rails and blew back on the decks. Nevertheless, the motors hummed and the ferry moved on.

A few larger-than-normal waves started rolling under the hull of the ferry. Sherman was surprised that the wind rose so quickly, but to all appearances it was only a summer squall. The ferry pushed on toward New London. Halfway across the Sound, the wind reached gale force. Winds now whistled about the ferry. Large, rolling waves rocked it. Sherman was glad that the voyage was half over. The weather had really taken a turn for the worse. Rarely had he seen it that bad.

By the time the ferry was three-fourths of the way across the Sound, Sherman knew he was in a dangerous situation. The suddenness of it disturbed him. Waves only seen in the worst North Atlantic storm were washing right over the decks of the ferry. From the howling of the wind, Sherman knew he was taking the ferry right through the teeth of a hurricane. Now, a ferryboat is never designed to encounter such weather. Its hull, decks, or superstructure are not meant to counter forty-foot waves and winds over 150 miles per hour. No one on board knew that better than Sherman.

He thought of what he could do. Essentially he had three choices: continue to New London, keeping the seas behind him; ride out the storm, but that meant turning the ferry in the waves, exposing it to more danger; or go back to Orient Point, which also called for a dangerous turning maneuver. A steamship built for the North Atlantic trade could safely turn around in this kind of situation. Its heavy steel platings, sealed portholes, and solid-steel compartment doors would protect it while turning during the perilous moments when the whole side of the ship would be exposed to the full brunt of oncoming waves. Sherman knew that there was only one choice: He had to go on to New London. He continued onward. The waves were so huge that the ferry was roller-coastering up and down them.

Of course by then the passengers knew of the danger. Whatever their fears, they never displayed them, though most silently prayed to be saved. Otherwise there was nothing to do except sit inside and listen as waves big enough to dent the armor plating of a heavy cruiser hit the ferryboat, then washed right through the open parts of it.

Finally Sherman saw land. He started looking for the New London smokestacks and rooftops that he always used for guides. He could not find them. Was he too far west? Too far east? With his binoculars he scanned the coast. How could he have made such a mistake, even in rough seas? Then he froze. Through his binoculars he saw the stump of a tall chimney. His landmarks had blown away! He adjusted course and headed toward the New London harbor.

The passengers, thankful that the journey was about to end, looked ahead. In a few minutes the nightmare voyage would be over. But as the ferry came around a headland, the passengers' fear increased instead of abated. New London was on fire. The whole city seemed to be burning. Clouds of smoke rolled away in the winds. Bright orange and yellow flames leaped into the sky.

Worse for the people on the ferry was the sight of the harbor. It was filled with sunken, battered, and broken ships. The waves and tides had thrown a lightship across the rails of the New London train station. A large four-masted sailing ship used by the Coast Guard as a training ship lay smashed and half sunken against a building. The city's wharves and piers were broken or under water. Huge waves rolled into low-lying parts of the city. And there were ships adrift. It was obvious that they could ram other vessels, sinking them.

To take the ferry into that harbor would have been suicidal. To begin with, there was not one dock where the passengers and crew could land. Such huge waves were washing over the already sunken docks that anyone disembarking would have been swept away and drowned. Worse, though, were the runaway ships. Some were so large that if they hit the ferry they would sink it.

Few people have ever been faced with as dreadful a choice as Captain Sherman was. There was only one thing he could do. He would have to risk turning the ferry around. For a few moments it would be broadside to waves powerful enough to smash open the strongest breakwaters. Even the captain of a battleship would have hesitated to make that choice. This was a clumsy ferry. But there was no other way out of the situation. Then, after turning the ferry around, the captain would have to keep it at sea, for it would be impossible to return to Orient Point safely against the wind. All night he would have to battle huge waves he could not even see in the darkness.

Sherman explained the situation to the crew and passengers. Everyone quietly accepted the news. There were no tears, no cries. There was only the stoic silence of agreement.

Sherman looked at the raging sea. Mountainous waves rolled

toward the ferry. Hissing winds tore the very tops off them. He knew that the waves came in series. A series of giants would be followed by a series of lesser waves. He studied them. A series of giants rolled under the stern of the ferry. The next series would be smaller waves. Even so, these smaller waves were larger than most captains ever see in the North Atlantic, which is noted for its huge waves. He ordered his helmsman to turn the ferry around, then he waited.

Slowly the ship turned in the wind. When it began to lurch in a strange way, the helmsman turned and looked at the captain. "Keep turning" was all Sherman said. A mammoth wave crashed against the side of the ship, which shuddered from stem to stern. The wave rolled under the keel. The ship turned more. Now it was broadside to the waves. An even larger wave towered over them. If it broke, that would be it. At the last moment the wave, still about to break, rolled under the ferry. The ship tilted crazily. Up and up went one side. Cars shifted; chairs slid across the decks and slammed into the wall. The gunwale went under water. Water poured through the open part of the vessel where the cars were stored. The ferry heeled over as far as she'd go without plunging downward to the bottom of the Sound. The turning propellers, lifted out of the water, made the metal plates of the deck vibrate like a sounding board.

Slowly the ship settled back the other way. It kept turning as it did so. The next wave looked even more threatening, but when it hit, the ship was already turned enough so the wave hit it only a glancing rather than fatal blow. Nevertheless, the vessel lurched strangely. It went up, askew on the wave, then its bow plunged into the water. The propellers sounded as though they would break as they again came out of the water. The ship settled back, turned more into the wind. The next wave hit almost head-on, but the immediate threat of being swamped was over. Sherman had safely gotten his ferryboat turned into the wind. By all odds, he should not have won this battle against the sea, but win he did.

There was still the battle of the night to look forward to. All night long, Sherman kept his ferry directly into the oncoming waves. Time and time again the ferry's bow would smash into the watery wall of a huge wave. All through the ship one could hear the thunderous roar of the battle. Too much strain and the seams in the hull would open. Throughout this ordeal the passengers were physically miserable. Seasickness was the least of it. Lacking food, warm drinks, and creature comforts, they could only passively await whatever end was in store. Spray and water leaked into all compartments. Wearing life jackets, the passengers had to sit upright all night, continually assaulted by the screech of the wind, the hiss of flying spray, the thunder of the waves, in addition to everything else. It was a horrible night of distress and silent fear.

Near dawn, the wind abated. It fell off almost as quickly as it had risen the day before. The waves pounding them now had less power in them. Gradually the people on board realized that they had won, that they would live. As miserable, bedraggled, and sick as they were, they smiled at each other. When light appeared in the sky and the sun's welcome rays reflected off the tops of the large waves still sweeping the Sound, the people gathered at the railing and looked about them.

Once more Sherman turned the ferry around. Now he could take it into New London's harbor. He wanted to dock there, but there was not one dock remaining. He had to dock in Groton, Connecticut, instead. Before anyone got off the ferry there, the captain, crew, and passengers stood in a circle with their arms linked on each other's shoulders and sang the Doxology:

> *Praise God, from whom all blessings flow;*
> *Praise Him, all creatures here below;*
> *Praise Him above, ye heavenly hosts;*
> *Praise Father, Son and Holy Ghost.*

The Catskill was not the only ferryboat to be threatened with disaster that night on the Sound. A larger, more powerful ferryboat—the *Park City*, which routinely made the trip between Port Jefferson, New York, and Bridgeport, Connecticut—also skirted disaster. It left Port Jefferson at 2:00 P.M. on the twenty-first and headed north for Bridgeport.

Soon the *Park City* too was in heavy seas. Even though she was 150 feet long and sturdily built, there were problems. The captain, Ray Dickerson, decided to turn the ship in the heavy seas, just as Sherman had done with his vessel. But though the *Park City* was much larger and heavier than *The Catskill,* he could not complete the maneuver. The winds and seas were too much. He decided to lower the heavy anchors. He hoped they would grab the bottom and swing the ship around, so it would face into the wind. They did not grab. The water was too deep, and the ship drifted instead. That was all right, as far as the captain was concerned, for he knew that sooner or later the anchors would touch bottom and hold. But there was one worry. It was possible that the ship would drift to a shoreline where the water was deep. If so, the ship could break up on the rocks.

At first things were under control. Then a situation of terrifying danger developed. Mountainous waves were breaking over the bow, and water began to get into the engine room. Seamen kept the engines going and the ship's pumps shot water out of the ship. But no matter how hard the pumps worked, they could not keep up with the flood. By 3:15 P.M. the water reached the boilers. There was a great hissing sound as seawater swamped them. The ship was without power, helplessly adrift on the Sound.

The crew tried to work hand pumps. But even as they worked them, they knew they could not keep up with the water entering the ship. Able-bodied male passengers, who only an hour and a half before had no other thoughts than of a routine arrival in Bridgeport, were soon also manning the pumps. The water level in the engine room rose notwithstanding. Before long both crewmen and male passengers were in waist-deep water.

Other passengers sat in their cars and passively awaited

whatever fate would bring them. Darkness came and the ship tossed on the waves. The wind seemed to be trying to claw the superstructure off, whistling and screaming as it hit railings and the masts.

The night was dreadful. Unguided and unpowered, the ship lurched, rolled, and pitched its way through the seas. Thirty-foot waves towered over it time and time again to come crashing down on its sides. Passengers were sick with fear. The water kept rising in the engine room. Men working the pumps had to retreat. The water was above the five-foot mark.

In the meantime, both company offices in Port Jefferson and Bridgeport had put out a bulletin that the ship was missing. The Coast Guard, already searching for dozens of sinking ships and drowning people, said they would look out for it.

Well into the evening, a sudden, huge shudder went through the ship. A frightening jolt was felt from stem to stern. The metal plates of the deck and hull groaned. Most thought the end had come, but it was actually the anchors finally grabbing bottom that they felt. The ship began to swing into the wind, a safer position. The captain knew that some of his problems were solved. But he did worry that another ship could plow into them in the darkness.

Water continued rising in the engine room. At five and a half feet deep it reached the electrical equipment, and the ship was plunged into darkness. This was almost too much for the passengers. Cowering in their cars, they were again sure the end had come for them. It was terrible enough to spend the night at sea in such a storm, but to do so in utter darkness was almost too much. Luckily, crewmen eventually found a few kerosene lamps. Emergency running lights were turned on, but they were weak. The captain knew that ships in the wind and rain could hardly see them.

Then to the utter relief of everyone, water came into the ship in smaller amounts. The hand pumps started to win the battle against the seawater. More water was being pumped out of the ship than came in. The captain assured all that they would survive the night.

The next morning the *Park City* was found by the Coast Guard cutter *Galatea,* which towed the stricken ferry to Port Jefferson. The cutter radioed ahead that it was bringing in the *Park City* and a crowd of over a thousand cheering, weeping, laughing people was on hand to meet the ferryboat.

While the ferryboats struggled through that harrowing night, another ship and crew did too. Permanently anchored in the Sound was the lightship *Cornfield.* Its light, which burned on a tower above the decks, marked the location of the dangerous Cornfield Reef. Unlike other ships, lightships do not have engines and propellers. They are supposed to stay put and are held in place by heavy anchors. If they must be taken to a harbor, they are towed there by tugs.

Unlike most people in the hurricane, who had the option of escaping it, the crew of ten men on the *Cornfield* knew that they had to face any bad weather where they were, no matter how dangerous it got. In the early afternoon of the twenty-first, when the winds began to pick up, the crew methodically prepared the ship for rough weather. The ship was built in such a way that the interior could be made quite watertight, thanks to heavy steel doors that could be screwed shut. Outer portions of the ship were not as strongly built. By the time the really mountainous waves were upon them, the crew had finished securing all they could on the decks and on the outer portion of the ship. The speed with which they did their work no doubt saved them.

Though the ship weighed 197 tons and was 115 feet long, it was not the best ship to be in during a hurricane. In a severe wind and with huge seas breaking over it, the ship could only buck against the chains of its huge anchors. The effect in heavy seas was that the chains would actually keep the ship from riding up with the waves. Buffeted by huge waves, it could actually

The New England hurricane of 1938 caused widespread damage. At Scarsborough, Rhode Island, people search through ruined buildings for their belongings. *National Archives*

be held several feet under water. Sure enough, within a short time after the storm rose, the ship was beginning to plow downward, for that was the apparent effect. Green water was rising over it. The crew, seeing what they were in for, decided to retreat to the watertight interior compartment. But that was a dreadful choice, for all they could do there was to bottle themselves up helplessly and wait out the storm. As the full fury of the storm hit, the men sat trapped in the bowels of the lightship. The waves rolled right over it. Held captive by its anchors, the ship seemed to dive into the turbulent water. For long moments the decks were as much as twenty feet under the surface. The men could hear the groaning of the steel hull plates. They stared at the bulkheads—even a small crack there could doom them. The storm gained strength. The wind rose and waves became larger. The noise was unbelievable. The men could hear outside portholes popping, rails being ripped away. Then came the most frightening noise. The anchors were actually dragging. The

helpless crew could do nothing as the winds and waves began to carry the ship away. At some point, the powerful waves would beat the ship to pieces on the shore. The men would drown.

The anchors were dragged for miles. Then they grabbed again. The winds finally died down. Late in the morning when the storm had ceased, the men unscrewed the heavy steel inner compartment doors and went out on deck. Skylights were gone. The outer hull was filled with water. Lifeboats were crushed, rails torn off the ship, metal twisted into noodle shapes. But the men were alive. A few hours later a ship came by to rescue them.

In Connecticut and Rhode Island the hurricane literally wiped out small towns and beach resorts near the Sound and ocean. Within hours there was a large death toll. Some people survived terrifying ordeals. The Geoffrey Moore family of Watch Hill, Rhode Island, lived through an almost unbelievable experience.

Early in the morning on the day of the hurricane, Mr. Moore suffered a heart attack. His wife, naturally concerned about his condition, telephoned a doctor. The doctor advised her to keep Mr. Moore in bed all day. Mrs. Moore, her four children, and three family employees settled down for a quiet, restful, uneventful day.

As Mr. Moore rested in bed, the wind began to rise. Once up, it quickly rose to hurricane force. Before long, huge waves were beating against the house. The children, looking out the window, were amazed to see a nearby house go crashing down in the wind. A few minutes later a neighbor, Jim Nestor, clad only in his underwear, appeared at their door. Mrs. Moore asked where his family was. They were gone, he told them. Dead!

Now fully aware of the immediate danger, everyone huddled together in what appeared to be the strongest part of the house. Sure that he would die, Mr. Moore told his wife good-bye. She told him not to give up yet. Just then the house started to buckle. As it sank downward, everyone raced upstairs to avoid being crushed in the downstairs rooms. All got there safely, but they were trapped under the attic roof, which now lay almost on the ground.

The children wondered aloud if they would die. Mrs. Moore was certain that the end had actually arrived for them all. It seemed only a matter of time before the sea battered the house to pieces or they were drowned. She quietly and firmly told the children to say their last prayers. The children took rosaries and with their mother went through the Act of Contrition. The adults, seeing the children's bravery and calmness, were given renewed courage.

At the end of the attic was a window. Because it was closed, it had kept out the water rising above it. Mr. Moore decided they might be able to escape if he broke it and they swam out one by one. He smashed it. A torrent of seawater rushed into the attic. The force of the water was so great that nobody could even get near the window, much less swim out against the onrushing water. Things had taken a turn for the worse. In minutes they would be drowned. Waist deep in the water, all felt a certainty they'd never see each other again. The water rose rapidly. Outside the wind screamed.

Just then a tremendous gust roared out of the storm. The attic shook under the sudden impact. There was a wrenching sound. Shingles and timbers came apart overhead and flew away in the wind. To their joy, the group saw daylight and scudding clouds above them. There was a hole. Quickly they all climbed up and through it to the rooftop. Fortunately for them, there were several pipes sticking up out of the roof. They held onto them, hoping that they could cling to the roof until the winds ceased and the waters receded.

To their distress, the roof began to move. Within minutes it was floating away on the waves of a wild sea. The frightened storm victims had no idea where they were going. They lost all sense of location in the driving rain, spray, and wind. Occasionally they saw other roofs, telephone poles, furniture, mattresses, and clothing float by. But in what direction were they going? Were they going to sea? They could not tell. Young Geoffrey pointed to the water and yelled. There were sharks circling about, confirming their fear that they were headed out to sea.

After a long time, they saw a buoy next to them. They recognized it. Much to their relief, they were not going out to sea after all, but were headed across the Napatree Bay. But their worries were not over. The roof they were on was coming apart. It was only a matter of time before it would be a loose mass of timbers and shingles. All around them were boards with nails and window frames with daggerlike glass splinters in them. To be in the water would mean one would be cut to ribbons. There was nothing to do but to hang on. And so they did, while the rain pelted them and waves breaking on the edge of the roof turned to spray that flew into their faces. Then the roof began to split apart. From deep within the remains of the attic they heard their doomed-to-drown parrot call out "Polly want a cracker." Once more their end looked to be near.

Just as the roof was breaking up, the winds drove it ashore on Barn Island. Amazingly, they had landed safely. The marooned group searched for other people, without success. Night was falling and the air was getting cold. No one was dressed for this ordeal. Mr. Moore had on a woolen shirt, but the waters had shrunken it until it was the size of a child's sweater. They all began to shiver and shake. Since there was no kind of shelter, they had a new fear—that they would die of exposure.

Against all odds, they had another stroke of luck. Near an old wall they discovered a haystack. It seemed strange that the wind had not blown it all away. They dug down into the heart of the hay and huddled together for warmth. Every now and then, one of them would poke his or her head out of the hay- stack to look about. One time they saw a flashlight beam. They hollered and called, but the light disappeared. They never knew who had the light. What was the person doing there on the island? Did whoever it was live or die?

During the night they saw a very strange sight. To the west, part of the sky was lit with huge flames. They painted the mov- ing clouds orange and red. The reflected light on the clouds wavered, alternately bright and dim. They could not imagine where the fire was or what was burning. It was the New London fire.

Shortly after dawn, a boatman came to the island and res- cued the tired, bedraggled, but amazingly fortunate people. Surprisingly, at no time during the ordeal did Mr. Moore's heart give him any trouble. So much for a day in bed.

But while some survived, others were dying. One of the sad- dest events was the death of several schoolchildren near James- town, Rhode Island. The hurricane hit just after school let out and the children were waiting for the bus to pick them up. Mr. Norman Caswell, the school bus driver, got there on time, and the children entered the bus. To get the children home, Caswell had to drive the bus across a causeway. Even during normal high tides water rose almost to the top of it. As Caswell approached the causeway, the tides, pushed higher by the hurricane, were already washing over it. Because of the direction of his approach, he apparently never saw how high the water was.

Joseph Mateos saw the danger from the other side of the causeway and tried to stop the bus by signaling to it. Mr. Mateos, worried by the high winds and rising seas, had driven toward the school to pick up his four children, but when he arrived at the causeway, he saw it was flooded. Worse, he witnessed a car being washed off of it. Two people in the car drowned in front of his eyes. As the bus approached the causeway from the other side, Mateos frantically signaled it to stop. The bus, however, kept rolling until it too was on the causeway. Mateos, knowing his own children were on the bus, could only watch and pray that nothing would happen.

When the bus got halfway across the causeway, it stopped. The wind rose and huge waves rolled in from the sea. In minutes they'd washed the bus off the causeway. It slid into deeper water. For a while its roof could be seen above the waves.

Caswell, realizing that the rising water would soon drown all the children, opened the bus door and one by one placed them on the roof. If the storm had been letting up, they could perhaps have waited it out and been rescued. The storm's fury, however, was increasing at a rapid rate.

Caswell knew that if they waited on the bus roof any longer they would certainly die. He decided to help the children swim to safety. He told the strongest and oldest of them, Clayton Chellis, to hold the hands of children at the end of a line they were forming. Caswell took the hands of the children at his end of the line. He and the eight children then lowered themselves into the raging waters.

Mateos watched his four children and the others enter the waves. They moved away from the bus just in time. Large waves washed over the top and it disappeared. He saw heads bobbing up and down. Then out of the sea rose a gigantic wave. Mateos stared helplessly at the mountain of water racing toward the causeway. As it moved over the children and Caswell, they all disappeared.

Mateos watched the waves one after the other roll over the place where they had all vanished. There was no sign of any of them. Then, out of the corner of his eye, he saw a man float ashore. He raced to him. It was Caswell. He shook him. Caswell begged him to let him die. He had lost all the children, he said, and he did not want to live. Mateos helped him, but Caswell nevertheless died shortly afterward. Most people felt he died of a broken heart.

Only one child survived, Clayton Chellis. Some time later witnesses reported seeing a body—they thought of one of the other children--drifting out to sea. They were not sure. At any rate, the others were never seen again.

For some survivors, the aftereffects of a disaster may occur years later. Indeed, in some cases, the death of a person may be related directly to a disaster even if the death takes place years in the future. This seems to be the case with Chellis. His sister was one of the children on the bus who died. The impact of the experience never left him. Years later he drowned in a swimming pool in California. He was alone at the time. What happened? We can never really know, but it could be that his drowning in the pool was psychologically connected with the 1938 hurricane. When official death tolls are made up and published a short time after a disaster, this sort of death is never listed. Official death tolls only record the deaths that took place during a storm. They don't list the deaths from heartbreak,

WPA workers help people find their belongings at Oakland Beach, Rhode Island, after the New England hurricane of 1938 ravaged the seacoast. *National Archives*

those that result from long-term physical disabilities suffered in a storm, or later heart attacks, suicides, and psychologically motivated deaths.

The storm destroyed huge sections of the Connecticut and Rhode Island shores. Beach resort communities such as Horseneck Beach, Rhode Island, simply disappeared. Not one house remained there after the storm. In nearby Westport many houses were totally destroyed. People found themselves trapped in houses that were half under water. Twelve-year-old Ann Mills was in her house with the family maid, Mary Frances Black. The water rushed into the house so fast that they could barely keep ahead of it as they ran up the stairs. Fearing the house would go at any second, Ann decided to dive out the second-story window into the sea and swim away. As she did, she turned to Black and called to her to follow. The maid yelled that she did not know how to swim. Ann, already in the water, had no choice but to swim for land with the next wave. The maid hollered, "Good-bye, Ann!" The girl made it to shore, reached high ground, and lived. The remains of the house were later found miles away, deposited on a golf course. There was no sign of Miss Black. Her body was never found.

With a storm this extensive, it is very difficult to say which place suffered the most. Many people would probably say that Providence, Rhode Island, was hardest hit. Providence is located at the head of Narragansett Bay, which, because of the wind direction, served as a funnel for the waves and high tide to move into. Pushed up the narrowing bay by the winds, the waters simply piled up in and around Providence. Added to all that, of course, was the damaging impact of the high winds. Together these added up to disaster.

Prior to 1938 the worst storm in Providence's history was "the great gale" that hit the city on September 23, 1815. The winds of that storm had pushed water up Narragansett Bay, flooding the city. To mark that instance of high water, the city had erected a plaque indicating that during the height of the storm water levels had reached a line eleven feet nine and a quarter inches above mean high water. From 1815 until 1938 no comparable storm struck the city. But during the 1938 hurricane, seawater was five feet higher than the line on the plaque.

The water rose so fast that some witnesses say it looked as though it were pouring into the city after a dam had burst. Literally within minutes people drowned in cars as the water rose over the car roofs. Some people tried to stay in their cars, closing the windows and hoping for the best. Most of them died. Others swam for it and made it. Hundreds in the second stories of buildings watched helplessly as people below died in the swirling waters.

Near Turks Head Square in the middle of the city fifty people watched Chester Hayes drown. He clung to his automobile. People realizing that he did not know how to swim tried to get a rope to him. But he was swept away in the water before it reached him. Another man, seeing Hayes pulled away from his car, went into the swirling waters after him. Both disappeared forever.

Not only did the high winds push water into the city, but it set many ships loose as well. These drifting vessels threatened everything on the waterfront. They were like battering rams. They pounded other ships to pieces, battered wharves into pulpwood. A tugboat smashed into a railroad bridge, destroying it. Several families lived on houseboats. These sank. Many people, with their children in their arms, only barely made their escape in time.

The hurricane quickly knocked out the electrical power. Throughout the hurricane and all that night the city was in darkness. People caught on dark streets where the winds howled and brought down roofs, signs, and telephone poles were terrified. Others waited for nonexistent transportation. Hundreds gathered in Union Station to wait for trains that would never come. The ceiling high above the waiting crowd was made of glass set in a steel framework. The winds howled over the roof. Then a huge gust of wind broke it. Deadly pieces of glass showered down on the people below. Screaming, they ran for shelter. Dozens were badly cut by the glass. A similar glass ceiling over the reading room in the city's public library also shattered and fell.

In less than an hour, Providence was brought to an absolute standstill. Office workers were stranded in upper-story offices. Even if they could have taken the elevators, which were not running, what could they do when they got to the ground floor? Water blocked them from the street. Nothing moved on the streets. Submerged cars and buses were stalled. Since most rowboats and other craft were damaged, there were no rescue boats. And even if the office workers could have escaped from their buildings, what good would that have done? No transportation was working. Many just gave up and spent the night in their offices. Others stranded by the storm were not so lucky. They clung to trees, fire escapes, or other objects for hours, often exposed to the wind and rain that lashed the city.

As dusk fell, troops arrived. They turned on powerful search-lights to illuminate their way. The beams crisscrossed the sky or were aimed down streets. The piercing lights gave a surre-alistic nightmare effect to the scene.

After devastating southern Connecticut and Rhode Island, the hurricane roared northward. It destroyed houses along the Massachusetts coast, but also felled trees inland. Hartford, Connecticut, suffered significant damage.

At 6:15 on the evening of the twenty-first, girls of the North-field Seminary in Northfield, Massachusetts, were eating sup-per in a large dining hall. Outside they could hear the scream-ing wind of the hurricane hitting the roof and tree branches drumming against the walls. Unknown to them at the moment, a tall chimney next to the dining hall was beginning to topple in the wind.

The chimney suddenly snapped. Horrified girls looked up to see it crashing through the roof toward them. It sliced through the roof so cleanly that its outline was left in the timbers. One hundred and forty girls were in the hall at the time. They had but a split second to watch it. With a thunderous roar, it landed on top of several girls as the others, screaming in terror, ran for their lives.

Remarkably, for all that, only two girls were killed outright. Forty others were seriously injured. A biology teacher rushed to the aid of one girl lying on her back. So much blood was in the girl's mouth that she was choking to death. The teacher rolled her over so she could breathe, and thereby saved her.

The terrified girls, frightened that another nearby chimney might come crashing into the room, were herded into a base-ment. For hours they waited, wondering when the other chimney would fall. It never did. In the meantime, school workers took the injured girls to the infirmary, but that was soon full. Because all the telephone wires were down, they could not reach outside doctors. Some school workers tried to get through to a hospital in a car, but were blocked by fallen trees. They gathered crews of volunteers who, armed with hand saws, cut the trees that blocked the way. Slowly, painfully, they got through to tell the outside world of the school's plight.

The hurricane rolled on through the darkness. As it moved north it went overland. Denied the warm air of the seas, it lost power. Still, it had enough force to kick up huge waves on Lake Champlain. Some of the waves on the lake were larger than those seen in many Atlantic storms. The storm went through Montreal, knocking down chimneys, rolling garbage cans about. After that it veered a bit down to the west and disappeared into the north woods, where it died.

When New Yorkers and New Englanders dug out from under the wreckage of the huge storm, they counted 680 people killed. Forty-five hundred homes, cottages, and farm buildings had been completely destroyed. Many of the homes had predated the Revolutionary War. Some were huge mansions. Over fifteen thousand other homes, cottages, and farm buildings were gone. Farmers counted 1,675 head of livestock dead. Four hundred million dollars' worth of damage was done. In today's terms, that sum would be well over $1.5 billion.

5. Agnes: A Third-rate Killer

In terms of property damage, Tropical Storm Agnes would prove the worst storm in American history. Ironically, as storms go, Agnes did not begin life as much of anything. It became a killer and superdestructive through a set of unusual circumstances. From its very beginning, Agnes was a peculiar storm that constantly broke all the rules.

The National Weather Service discovered its first tropical storm of the 1972 season in mid-June. A large mass of rotating clouds and winds was moving off Cozumel Island, which lies just off Mexico's Yucatan coast. Because it was the first tropical storm of the year, it was labeled with a name beginning with A—Tropical Storm Agnes.

From then on the weather service kept track of it. Agnes first wandered north; it hesitated, then moved more or less eastward. As it moved in the Gulf of Mexico its winds gathered speed. They finally got up to 75 miles per hour, which made it officially Hurricane Agnes. It crossed over northern Florida. High winds battered Casey Beach. Clouds dumped flooding rains. The hurricane's wind speeds dropped sharply as it moved across land. By the time it reached the Atlantic Ocean, it was hardly a storm worth considering. Indeed, for a few days meteorologists more or less forgot about it as it meandered about over the Atlantic.

Over the warm waters of the Gulf Stream Agnes slowly began to build up once more, for moisture and heat are fuel to tropical storms and hurricanes. Hour by hour the storm grew. Even so, it never came close to becoming a hurricane again. It was just one big rainy tropical storm, filled with an incredible amount of moisture. Meteorologists later calculated that it carried enough water to fill a 134-square-mile lake one thousand feet deep.

Such an immense amount of water dumped anywhere on land was sure to cause floods. Nevertheless, even that amount of water, in itself, was not what made Agnes America's most damaging storm.

The trouble was that Agnes was headed straight for the northeast coast, where for days there had already been local flooding. Every river ahead of Agnes was running full; many were overflowing their banks.

On June 21, Agnes lethargically moved into eastern Virginia. There were no high winds, no rushing storm—nothing like that. There were just solid sheets of rain. Every gutter on every roof near Richmond, Virginia, spouted water. Streets soon became impassable. Within hours most major highways in eastern Virginia were blocked. Transportation simply stopped. The James River, already flooding, rose higher inch by inch. Officials sounded the alert, and people near the river, especially in low-lying areas, were told to evacuate. Within hours the worst flood ever seen on the James River was in progress. Several stone bridges spanned the river. The waters soon poured right over them, making large rapids on the downstream side. Whirlpools sucked in debris: lawn chairs, automobiles, trees. The bridges

17 JUNE 1972
TIME OF PHOTO 1800 GMT

AGNES

18 JUNE 1972
TIME OF PHOTO 1800 GMT

AGNES

19 JUNE 1972
TIME OF PHOTO 1800 GMT

AGNES

20 JUNE 1972
TIME OF PHOTO 1800 GMT

**21 JUNE 1972
TIME OF PHOTO 1800 GMT**

**22 JUNE 1972
TIME OF PHOTO 1800 GMT**

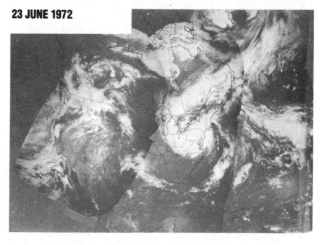

23 JUNE 1972

Satellite photographs of cloud cover show not only the shape of Tropical Storm Agnes, but its path from June 17 to 23, 1972. *National Oceanic and Atmospheric Administration*

could not withstand the force pushing against them. One by one they buckled. Thousands of people trying to flee the area were stranded. Automobiles were abandoned right and left.

Floodwaters got into the James River filtration plant that served the city of Richmond. The sewage-filled waters contaminated the city's drinking water. At about the same time electrical power failed, so that the capital city of Virginia was without both drinking water and electricity.

By some quirk of fate, a few days before the flood the state's National Guard had been testing powerful emergency filtration equipment designed for just such a contingency. The equipment had been set up near the river. As quickly as possible it was hooked into the water-supply system. But in the intervening hours people went thirsty. As night fell they had no lights or refrigeration; the water was rising in the streets. The governor of the state called for federal aid. He prepared and signed the necessary forms by the light of several flickering candles.

Soon floodwaters also inundated Alexandria, Virginia, a Washington, D.C., suburb. Water was up to the ceilings of the first-floor rooms of houses, offices, and factories. Successful evacuations saved hundreds of people. But fires broke out. One of the worst gutted the middle of the city's business district. Fire trucks could not get to it. The high waters in the streets would have stalled their engines. The firemen could only watch as orange flames leaped out of windows and spread across roofs. Columns of thick black smoke curled up into the sheets of rain. Fire and flood made an eerie combination.

The storm continued its movement north. Waters poured across the yard of the Pennsylvania governor's mansion in Harrisburg. Workmen, already weary from efforts to stem the flood, tried to save what they could. But the furnishings in the beautiful mansion were ruined. Carpets, furniture, and expensive art objects suffered serious water damage.

Night fell. Just to the north of Philadelphia waters swept

through Pottstown, Pennsylvania. The Schuylkill River had quickly flooded, and water raced unimpeded into the city. Electricity winked out. The water came so fast that many people had virtually no chance of escape. Frightened families climbed onto rooftops in the darkness. There they sat in pouring rain in the blackness of night. Just below them they could hear water breaking windows, floating furniture around, and cracking the foundations of their homes. Water climbed inexorably up toward them, a mortal threat that inched closer and closer.

Navy, army, and marine helicopters were ordered to Pottstown to rescue stranded people. Pilots, many of whom had war experience, soon realized that they were on a dangerous mission. Flying through pelting rain, they were forced to approach unseen houses below them in total darkness. These, of course, were surrounded by trees, telephone poles, and worst of all, high-voltage electrical transmission lines. But if help did not get to people soon, there would be a terrible loss of life. Pilots hovering over the city saw a weird sight below. In the darkness, tiny lights from candles and flashlights were winking up at them. Each light, no matter how small, indicated human life, a person threatened with death.

The pilots slowly, carefully, lowered their helicopters toward the stranded people. They strained their eyes trying to peer through the sheets of rain, watching out for electrical wires that could kill them. Somehow the pilots got above the rooftops, and then one by one they plucked people off the roofs of their homes. Some came aboard numbed with fear, some in hysterics, some sobbing, and some jubilant at being rescued.

The storm, which would end up dropping ten inches of rain in twenty-four hours, easily flooded the Susquehanna River. On its banks stood Wilkes-Barre, Pennsylvania, which would take the full brunt of the storm and suffer the worst damage from it.

The people of Wilkes-Barre knew a great deal about floods. In March 1936 a devastating flood rising to thirty-three feet above the normal height of the river had caused widespread damage to the city. Determined never to let that happen again, the citizens of Wilkes-Barre had built dikes near and around the city to hold back any future flood, even if it rose four feet higher than the 1936 flood. They were confident that the dikes could hold back anything in the way of floodwaters.

When the rains of Agnes poured into the Susquehanna River, it was already at flood stage; water lapped high up on the dikes. Heavy rains that had fallen a few days before had seen to that. During the night the water, greatly supplemented by Agnes, rose and rose. People began to have doubts about the dikes. Soon gangs of men, and some women, were hoisting bags of sand and placing them on top of the dikes. It was back-breaking work. The people worked in the driving rain under searchlights, lifting two-hundred-pound bags of sand. Weary, perspiring, soaked to the skin, the workers fought the flood, but it did no good at all. They may as well have spent the evening at the movies. All through the night they worked. A wail of sirens sounded in the morning. The sandbag crews stopped and looked at each other as they listened. The dikes had been breached!

Men, women, and children ran for their lives. Water shot over the dikes. Waterfalls of sewage-contaminated water poured down the sides of the dikes, which were quickly eroded away. The Susquehanna River poured into Wilkes-Barre.

Those who could ran for the high ground. Others had no choice but to climb onto their roofs. Passengers on one train caught by the water had no place to go but to the tops of the train cars.

Once more helicopters were ordered to the rescue. Because it was daylight the helicopter pilots had a much better time of it than at Pottstown. However, they were stunned by the scene below them. On little islands created by hilltops rising out of the water, large groups of people stood packed together. They reminded one pilot of wheat growing in a flooded field. Other pilots swooped down over city rooftops and began the job of picking people up there. Some people waved madly at them, others sat chain smoking, while still others huddled dejectedly under blankets.

Wilkes College, a small school in Wilkes-Barre, had for years been trying against great odds to build a good library and an up-to-date auditorium, with new pianos and a large new organ. They had finally gotten those by scraping together and pinching pennies and asking for donations. The organ alone had cost $35,000. Within a few hours, all that had so recently been achieved at such effort was washed away.

On the water rushed, isolating warehouses that caught fire as a result of electrical shortcircuits. The water around the burning buildings was deep—some boats were bumping into telephone wires strung twenty-five feet above the ground! The fire department had no way in the world of getting to the fires. They burned freely, consuming millions of dollars worth of merchandise. A pall of acrid, foul-smelling smoke hung over the city.

The floodwaters were filthy. Sewers emptied their contents upward. Garbage floated everywhere. In addition, most of the water was covered with a scum of oil and gasoline. The city was a disgusting swamp. Making it worse was the black smoke mixing with the rain.

The floodwaters poured into the large graveyard at Forty Fort on the northern edge of the city. Graves opened up. Caskets, skeletons, and partly decomposed bodies were added to the mess. One witness reported a wave of water carrying a line of floating coffins that looked for all the world like surfboards. Among the dead floating in the waters were the remains of the famous poet Elinor Wylie. Troops from the Graves Registration Section of the U.S. Army were immediately rushed to Forty Fort. The soldiers had the dreadful job of collecting the corpses, identifying them, and getting them back into their proper graves. The scene of these troops, wet to the skin in the rain and wading through the water carrying corpses, looked like something out of Dante's *Inferno*.

People waiting on rooftops soon discovered they were not the only creatures fighting for their lives. Countless rats that had been living in secret holes and corners of the city were also scrambling for their lives. People already in distress saw hordes of beady-eyed rodents coming at them. In spite of efforts to scare the rats away, many attacked people. Among those treated for rat bites were some who were badly injured. The worst cases were flown out to hospitals in Harrisburg.

Many pets died—cats, dogs, horses, goats, and other animals. Others were rescued. A few lone people sitting on rooftops had only Fido or Tabby to keep them company while they waited to be rescued. Moreover, dogs and cats helped keep the threatening rats at bay. Several of the animals that were rescued were sent to Lakehurst, New Jersey. Included among those pets and valuable farm animals were, oddly enough, two ducks.

Wilkes-Barre was virtually paralyzed. Temporary morgues were set up. Waterlogged goods of all varieties quickly rotted. Drinking water was in such short supply that two nearby breweries ceased canning beer and canned clean drinking water instead. Army transport planes flew in food, blankets, and medicines. Hundreds of mobile homes were towed to the area so that homeless people would have shelter.

The rescue operations went on for days. At first helicopters and later boats cruising the flooded city streets picked up stranded people. Some people had to wait for days before being taken to safety. One woman, fifty-nine years old and suffering from a heart condition, waited alone for thirteen days before she was rescued. Though she had known about the evacuation order, she had decided to stay in her house, for she could not imagine where she was supposed to go. The waters that invaded her house forced her to climb to the second story. There she had some canned goods, raw potatoes, and some raw green beans. Even though she lacked water and heat, she managed to survive

Wilkes-Barre, Pennsylvania, flooded by rains from Tropical Storm Agnes. *Official U.S. Coast Guard Photo*

on the liquids in the canned goods and on the potatoes and beans, which she ate raw. Several times during that period, people in boats saw her. They asked if she was all right. Each time she smiled and waved at them. But she was trapped. Even when the water went down, she could not get to the ground floor, for the stairs were deeply buried in thick, slippery mud. Afraid of falling, she stayed put. After thirteen days, some telephone men came to the door. They were amazed to learn the truth of her situation. Police came to take her to a hospital. She was reluctant to go, insisting everything was okay. She proved to have come through everything none the worse for the wear.

Wilkes-Barre was not the only place suffering severe damage. Farther south, in Nelson County, Virginia, the Chesapeake and Ohio Railroad's tracks were under water. People could only be rescued by helicopter. Hundreds escaped, but eleven died. There were so many power failures that half a million people were without electricity.

Dams throughout the region were threatening to break. Because water was pouring over the tops of nearby dams, twenty thousand people were evacuated from Elmira, New York. Near Big Flats, New York, a dam did break. Six thousand fled for their lives as water gushed out. People in Rochester, New York, were given the chilling news that the large Mount Morris Dam on the Genesee River probably would not be able to hold. Army engineers saved it by opening sluice gates. Millions of gallons of water shot down a river that was already flooding. The extra water caused a great deal of damage, but it was nothing compared to what would have happened if the dam had broken. If that had occurred, thousands would have drowned.

The town of Wellsville, New York, was entirely cut off. Residents were totally dependent on helicopters, and many owed their lives to the little choppers and brave pilots.

In Corning, New York, home of the famous Corning Glass Works, four large bridges spanning the Chemung River collapsed. The great glass works were under water. So was most of the city. Raging, angry waters destroyed buildings right and left. To make things worse, throngs of sightseers came to see the stricken city and the drama of its destruction. They stood on nearby hills and gawked at the scene below them, thrilled by the sight of the widespread destruction.

The situation was precarious. The city had no gas, no electricity, and worst of all, no drinking water. To avoid typhoid, people were told to boil all drinking water. People living in the worst areas were given free typhoid shots. Food did not arrive for days. Many people, seeing the Corning Glass Works under water, thought it would surely close. However, the chairman of the board of the Corning Glass Company got on the radio and reassured listeners that the firm would never leave Corning. Moreover, he offered $1,000 in interest-free cash loans to any past or present employee who suffered from flood damage.

The floodwaters were so great in quantity that several days after the storm they turned the normally brackish waters of the Chesapeake Bay into fresh water. The waters remained fresh long enough to kill most of the famous blue crabs in the bay, as well as many other types of shellfish and fish. Fishermen in Maryland were soon without a means of making a living. Had it not been for federal government grants, they would have had to leave the area to seek employment elsewhere. The fishing industry would have died and not been reestablished for decades. Fortunately, the fishermen did wait for nature to slowly heal itself. When the waters became brackish again, the crabs and other animals native to the bay eventually returned and multiplied.

On land, things returned to normal at a slow pace. For weeks Wilkes-Barre was a desolate city. People appeared to have a strange lassitude of a type that doctors and social workers had only seen during wars. Hotels that could have opened stayed closed. For weeks bars served drinks in paper cups. People seemed to lack the willpower even to do small things. The streets were muddy and dirty, and it took weeks to clean them. A peculiar odor hung in the air, a mixture of sewage, oil, wet plaster, mildew on wood, and plain old rot. It took time—plenty of time—but huge sections of the city were eventually rebuilt, and vitality returned to the people. Recovery was slow and painful.

In terms of property damage, no storm in America's history

even compares with Agnes's damage. It destroyed $3 billion worth of property. Twenty-five cities and towns were badly damaged, and some of those were totally destroyed. Three hundred thirty thousand people lost their homes. Moreover, the rains destroyed corn crops in large parts of Pennsylvania and in most of New York State. Two hundred thousand people had to be rescued from drowning. It was probably the biggest rescue operation in history. A million and a half pounds of food were parachuted into the Wyoming Valley, where Wilkes-Barre is located. About the same amount was dropped in all other areas. Thousands were given emergency medical treatment. In all, 118 people died. The death toll was kept down by warnings, the helicopters, and massive aid given by thousands of volunteers. All in all, this was one of the worst American storms, ironically just a third-rate tropical storm by most standards. Had it not been for a very strange set of circumstances, no one would ever have remembered Agnes.

6. The Great Tornado of March 18, 1925

America's most deadly single tornado ravaged the Midwest on March 18, 1925. In a few hours this one killer storm completely wiped out several towns, killed 689 people, left over 3000 severly injured, and caused millions of dollars of damage.

Tornadoes are nature's most violent storms. Though they can occur almost anyplace on earth aside from the polar regions, they occur most frequently in North America, especially in the Great Plains area. The most susceptible areas include northern Texas, all of Oklahoma, all of Kansas, and southeast Nebraska. Tornadoes appear most frequently in the springtime.

For a tornado to develop in a Plains state, three things are needed. First, a cold, dry polar air mass from Canada or the Rocky Mountain region must be moving in rapidly, at speeds of about 50 miles per hour. Second, a marine tropical air mass from the Gulf of Mexico or Pacific Ocean must be moving northward or northeastward over the plains. The temperature of the marine tropical air mass must be at least 75°F at the ground level, and the air must be very humid. Third, jet stream winds, 7 to 8 miles overhead, must be moving toward the east at 150 miles per hour or faster. When these three conditions are met a tornado may occur.

Most meteorologists think that when a cold polar air mass plows into the warm, moist tropical air mass at speeds of 50 miles per hour or more, the impact is so great that cold air actually spills up over the marine tropical air and effectively traps some of it below. An inversion is formed over many miles, with the cold air putting a lid on the warm air below. The warm, moist air, much lighter than the cold dry air above, naturally has a tendency to rise, but the cold air blocks it. Eventually, however, the warm, moist air punches holes in the overlying cold air and escapes into the atmosphere above. In doing so, a tall column of warm air rises rapidly.

The force of the rising, warm moist air is very great, and it frequently produces severe thunderstorms. This air, shooting upward, cools rapidly, and torrential rains start to fall. The lightning and thunder is much more severe than with most thunderstorms. Just before tornadoes, people frequently spot unusually large thunderstorms, which are often accompanied by severe hailstorms.

All along where the two air masses meet, there will be a line of violent thunderstorms.

Many meteorologists think that the jet stream, high above, racing along at very high speeds, gives the tall columns of rising warm air their twisting motion. Once they get this initial twisting motion, the whole column of air starts rotating around and around. This alone, according to these meteorologists, is enough to produce a tornado.

Other meteorologists, however, think that the rotating mass of air is, at first, quite wide, covering several square miles. As the air at the center continues to rise, often at faster and faster speeds, the whole rotating mass of air shrinks. In doing so, the mass rotates much faster, for it preserves its angular momentum.

To understand this, consider an example of how angular momentum is kept. If a skater rotates with her arms outstretched, she will move around rather slowly. But if she quickly pulls her arms inward, close to her body, she will spin around and around at high speed. Exactly the same principle holds true for the air mass. As it shrinks to a smaller rotating diameter, the air speed progressively becomes faster until a tornado has formed.

Since large and exceptionally brilliant lightning strokes are seen frequently in and around tornado funnels, some scientists have suggested that the heat of the lightning powers a tornado. Computer models have shown that lightning can help a tornado to form. After it has developed, however, the computer shows that the electrical discharges from lightning tend to weaken the tornado until it breaks apart. So no one knows exactly what role lightning plays. Most scientists tend toward the theory that it helps power tornadoes as they are born.

Another theory states that the thunderstorms themselves rotate and that tornadoes are nothing more or less than an outcome of these storms. This theory at least explains why tornadoes are almost always found in or near thunderstorms.

As it stands, no one knows what really happens. Naturally, it is very difficult for meteorologists to study tornadoes. To begin with, there is no way for a meteorologist to get instruments into a tornado and out again without them being smashed to pieces. To date, every single weather instrument caught in a tornado has been torn apart. Second, the odds are over a thousand to one against a tornado occurring in any given place, even in Texas, Kansas, or Oklahoma. It is possible that meteorologists will never have an opportunity to measure events inside of a tornado.

So, all the theories so far remain as theories. Even so, scientists are slowly understanding a bit more about tornadoes through such devices as radar, which spots them and helps measure wind speeds. Scientists have obtained other evidence, too. A tornado hit one of the towers on some transmission lines in Massachusetts. Engineers, who knew exactly how much stress the tower could have withstood, examined the damage and were able to state that the winds had reached a speed of at least 335 miles per hour.

Once a tornado develops, it usually moves from southwest to northeast at a speed of from zero miles per hour to 70 miles per hour. The funnel, from 800 to 2000 feet long, has a diameter at the base of about 200 to 330 yards. The path along the ground varies a great deal. Some tornadoes touch down and cover only a few feet of ground. Others have traveled across the ground for several hundred miles.

Though most photographs show tornado funnels to be black, of themselves they are actually not black at all. They are white or gray, because they are made up only of wind and rain. They become black only when they pick up dirt and dust from the ground.

Amazingly, several people have actually looked up inside a tornado's funnel and lived to tell about it. They have reported that constant lightning flickers along the inner edge of the funnel. They have noted that the air at the center of the funnel is clear and clean, even though dust and debris is seen swirling around the inside edge of the funnel.

Scientists have made computer models of tornado funnels in which the outside air is rising at about 200 miles per hour, while clean, cold air is falling at about the same speed down the center of the funnel. The computer models indicate that there probably are really two funnels, one inside the other. Where does the cold air come from? It pours in from the cold polar air mass high above, right down into the swirling funnel, while warm, moist air rises around the edges of the funnel.

A tornado funnel races across farmlands near Plainville, Texas, May 27, 1978. Its classic shape is clearly seen. *National Oceanic and Atmospheric Administration*

According to all accounts, March 18, 1925, was an exceptionally warm, muggy day. Warm, moisture-laden air masses from the south had moved into the Midwest corn belt. But farther north, cold air masses were rushing southward. Perfect tornado weather. Today, if meteorologists saw such conditions they would issue tornado warnings. But that day there were no tornado warnings. On that day, people seemed far more interested in the coming spring and the freedom from the winter's cold. No one realized the imminent danger, not even the Weather Bureau.

Late in the afternoon the United States Weather Bureau, as it was then still called, predicted thunderstorms in the tristate area of Indiana, Illinois, and Kentucky. The report pleased most people, for the sound of distant thunder is a sure sign that summer is on its way. There was not one mention by the Weather Bureau of tornado danger. Of course, in those days meteorologists lacked satellite photos, high-speed computers, high-altitude balloons, airplanes, and other sophisticated weather-monitoring devices.

Unknown to anyone, a tornado was brewing. Professor Henry J. Cox, a government forecaster in Chicago, later stated that the tornado developed in the Gulf of California. Once formed, it moved high above the ground in a northeasterly direction toward Arkansas. There its funnel first dipped downward toward the ground. It touched a few fields but did no damage. The base of the funnel ascended back into the clouds. It moved into southeastern Missouri.

When the funnel started coming down again, it was a white-gray color. It had not yet picked up the dust and other debris that make a funnel black. The funnel descending toward the ground outside of Annapolis, Missouri, is still thought to be the largest ever seen, any time, any place.

At a little after one o'clock in the afternoon, the monstrous, howling, writhing cone touched the ground just outside of Annapolis. It moved toward the town. The funnel turned black and ugly as it sucked up dirt, trees, barns, fences, and all else in its path. To the astonishment of the people who saw it, the tornado aimed right for Annapolis's only major street—Main Street. The town was surrounded by wooded hills on all sides. A tornado going there could do little or no damage. But instead of heading for the hills, this one bore down on Main Street. There was something uncanny and sinister about that. But residents had little time to ponder the situation. In minutes the twister hit. It roared right down the middle of the street, demolishing every single building on it in seconds.

W. C. Gunter, the railroad station agent, was sitting in his office at the depot when the tornado arrived. He was not thinking about much of anything when he looked out the window. Suddenly there it was—a huge tower of rotating black air loomed over the small depot. It seemed to come out of nowhere, like an apparition.

Gunter was more astonished and puzzled than frightened. He stood up and went to the window, a dangerous thing to do, for one of the great dangers from a tornado can often be flying glass, which will cut a person to ribbons. Oddly enough, some trick of the wind saved the window. It remained intact even as the rest of the depot collapsed. The walls and roof crumbled and buried a group of people in the waiting room.

Gunter spun around. The depot was gone. People trapped in the wreckage were screaming. Worse, a stove fell over, and fire began to spread through the wreckage. It appeared the fire would soon burn the trapped people alive. The screams were pitiful.

Gunter knew there were buckets for water for just such an emergency in the waiting room. But he knew he could never dig down to them through all the wreckage. What could he do? Suddenly he thought of using the drawers of his desk. He grabbed the largest, filled it with water, and began fighting the fire. Miraculously, he was able single-handedly to put out the blaze. Thanks to his inventive thinking, the injured people were saved from a more terrible fate.

The tornado left Annapolis and headed for Cape Girardeau. It plowed right into a public school just minutes after the children and teachers had left it.

The tornado moved on across the plains. It did some relatively minor damage to other towns, then headed straight for Murphysboro, Illinois, with a population of eleven thousand people and located in the center of an agricultural district. The huge, black, slithering tornado swayed in the wind. Those who heard it said it had the sound of a thousand freight trains. As it entered the town's residential district, houses simply disappeared. The force of the wind was so great that it snapped trees off near their base and actually jerked water pipes right out of the ground.

Charles Biggs was driving his car when he saw it. He knew what to do. He stopped his car and ran into the narrow ditch along the road. Such ditches usually provide some safety and are the best places to be if one is caught in open country. While Biggs huddled there in the ditch, he saw the tornado hit his car. The car rolled over, bounced down the road as though it were a basketball, and then popped up inside the tornado. It was never seen again.

Biggs was cut, but able to walk. He got out of the ditch and walked home. When he arrived there, he gasped. His house was a pile of matchwood. He walked into the wreckage. His daughter-in-law was sitting there. He started talking to her. She started to answer him, but died before his very eyes. She did not even look hurt.

He went to find the rest of his family. His two granddaughters had been thrown to the side of the house. They were dead. He found his wife and his mother. They, too, were dead. He pulled up some boards. Under them was his son. Dead. Near his son lay his daughter, who had just celebrated her sixteenth birthday. She too was dead. Too shocked for grief, he stood there in a daze. He could not think. Then he realized he was being shaken by a hand. It was his other daughter. She had just arrived home from school. Of the family, only the two of them had survived.

As the tornado roared through Murphysboro, it ripped away house after house. On the railroad tracks in town stood some huge locomotives. The wind funnel threw them around as though they were toys. Nothing was so large, so secure, that it could withstand the force of that tornado.

It is difficult to comprehend such power. Several incidents reveal its awesome strength. When the tornado ripped through the Reverend H. W. Abbot's house, it picked up some of his calling cards, which had been laid out on a table. Several days later one of those cards was found in Palestine, Illinois, 210 miles away.

The tornado swept through town killing some people, burying

others under debris. Not all the deaths occurred immediately. The piles of wood—collapsed houses, fallen trees, smashed boards—began to burn. Flames sprang up everywhere, and soon most of the city was on fire. Orange flames licked out of the wreckage, and columns of smoke rose above the stricken city.

The fire department was helpless to do much. Because the tornado had broken the water mains, the firemen could not find a hydrant with any water pressure in it. Even had they been able to get water, they could not get to most sections of the city. Everywhere trees, smashed vehicles, and other wreckage blocked the roads. The firemen did what they could, but the flames spread rapidly through the dry kindling that had moments before been homes. Trapped people were being burned alive. Most could not be aided. When it was all over, 210 people in Murphysboro had either been killed outright by the tornado or burned to death. Five hundred others were severly injured.

From all evidence, the gigantic tornado actually grew in size and power after smashing through Murphysboro. Packing stupendous power, it marched toward De Soto, Illinois, a small farming center with a population of six hundred people.

Usually it is very difficult to get an unobstructed view of a tornado in open country. However, several people in De Soto saw the tornado in the distance as it bore down on the town. One of those who saw it was F. M. Hewitt, a state senator.

Hewitt was making a business call on a woman who lived on the outskirts of town. They were talking in a room, when through the windows they saw the sinister funnel. Hewitt and the woman, who was carrying her six-week-old twins, went outside to see it more clearly. In the distance clouds appeared to be boiling in the sky. From Hewitt's description these were probably mammatocumulus clouds, so called because they have breast-shaped bulges hanging down from them. Rising and falling, these could easily give the appearance of a boiling cloud. In the center of these clouds was the tornado itself. Hewitt and the woman had no fear of it. They calmly watched it for a while. They even decided that the woman next door should see it too, so they got her. She came out with her baby and watched with them.

Lightning shivered across the sky, which now was dark as ink. The huge cone swayed slowly back and forth. Then they saw something that has rarely been seen by anyone. Floating high in the air ahead of the tornado were timbers, tree fragments, automobile parts—rubbish of all descriptions. These floated along on an updraft of air, seeming to defy gravity. They hovered in the air in dreamlike fashion.

Hewitt later described the roar as being somewhat like a wagon on a road. It is amazing in how many different ways the sound of a tornado has been described. People have likened it to the buzzing of millions of bees, to the roar of hundreds of locomotives, to the sound of jet engines.

As the tornado moved closer, Hewitt and the woman he was visiting decided to go indoors. Just as they got into the house, it slowly rose off the ground. They all jumped out of the house as it was lifted into the air. Outside, Hewitt felt himself being pulled straight up into the air, too. As he went up, he reached out and grabbed onto a post. He felt silly hanging onto the post, his legs flailing in the air. He wondered what people would think of him. Think? He saw others floating up into the dark clouds— with their houses. He saw the house he had just been in rise high into the air, then disintegrate. In seconds it was just an array of boards and shingles floating about.

And then it was all over. Hewitt's legs hit ground; he stood up. First he heard the cries of babies. Cries came from all directions. As he looked around he was surprised to see bodies everywhere. Most of the dead were old people or children. Many had their clothes completely ripped off them. Some were so covered with blood that they looked as though they'd been painted bright red from head to toe.

For a while Hewitt helped women hunt for their children. Then he found someone who was terribly injured, who would soon die. He went for help, but as he did so, he found someone else in worse shape. He forgot about the first person and ran for help for the second, but he found a third, a fourth, a fifth person, each seemingly worse than the others.

He stopped running. Was he the only person who was not hurt? The only one there who was not actually dying? Luckily, he soon saw another person, also unharmed, walking about in the ruins. He felt an overpowering joy to find another living person. He stayed near the other man and would not let him out of his sight. The two worked together helping people. Afterward Hewitt heard that the woman he was visiting had escaped injury. While Hewitt was near the edge of town helping people, the tornado was smashing its way into the center of town. Right in its path was the community's public school, filled with students and teachers. The massive black twister plowed into it. It lifted the roof with a great wrenching sound. Children screamed. Then the walls fell inward. Within seconds 125 students and teachers were buried in the wreckage. The scene was beyond belief. Screaming, dying children lay under the walls. Others were forced to witness their friends crushed, bleeding, their bodies torn, and to hear their dying screams.

As soon as they could, rescuers started digging the children out. But few of the rescuers actually came from De Soto, for most in the town were already dead or injured. Most of the people who helped come from nearby communities. One of those who was in the building but had survived was the principal. Though he was covered from head to toe with cuts and blood, he helped to direct the rescue operations.

As the dead children were taken from the school, they were laid out on the lawn under blankets to await identification by their parents. Many parents never showed up to identify their children— they were also dead.

One rescue worker saw two bleeding girls walking along a road not far from the school. Their clothes were in shreds. He went up to them and asked if they were from the school. They said they were. One explained that she had escaped the falling wall by jumping out the window. The other girl could not remember what had happened to her. All she knew was that one minute she was in the school and the next she was out on the road. He asked them where they were going. They could not answer him, for they had no idea where they were walking to or why they were on the road.

Of the 125 students and teachers in the school, 88 died. Almost all the others were badly injured.

The town of De Soto was gone. Not one building taller than ten feet high was left. The winds were so strong that roof beams were thrown fifteen miles away. Human bodies were tossed a mile away. Caught in every remaining tree, every standing fence, were tatters of clothing and shreds of human flesh. When the tornado hit the town, there were 600 people living there. It left behind 118 dead and 200 injured.

The black monster storm roared east into Frankfort, Illinois. One-third of that town's residential district was smashed in minutes. The tornado's noise was so loud and strong that it disoriented people and made them feel sick. They lost their sense of balance and became incapable of thought. Immediately after the tornado left there was an eerie silence. For quite a few seconds, there was no noise at all. And then the silence was broken by the screams, cries, and sobs of the wounded and dying. The tornado left 107 dead. Two hundred and fifty buildings were completely destroyed and damage was set at $2 million, a staggering figure in 1925.

And still the tornado plowed onward. It hit Gorham, McLeansboro, Parrish, Logan, Benton, Enfield, Bush, Thomsonville, Carmi, Crossville, Akin. It crossed over into Indiana and hit Princeton, Owensville, Griffin, Poseyville, and Elizabeth. Everywhere it left a trail of death, injury, grief, and hopelessness. Because it wiped out mine structures, factories, warehouses, and other commercial buildings, it left many without jobs.

All along the way, strange things happened. One railroad engineer, E. F. Shine of the Southern Railroad, looked down the tracks and to his amazement and consternation saw the tornado on the rails ahead. He knew he could not escape it. What should he do? He could stop the train, but that, he figured, would only give the tornado more time to damage it. His only hope, he thought, was to pull the throttle out and go full speed through the funnel.

He pulled it back for all he was worth. The train slowly gathered speed—40, 50, 60 miles per hour. The heavy train hurtled down the track, its great wheels pounding the rails. The black, opaque, whirling mass of death hovered there, waiting.

As the train sliced into the darkness of the tornado, Shine crouched down and grabbed onto the seat. Even above the noise of the racing locomotive, he could hear the horrible roar of the tornado. All went black. Above all the combinations of sounds, Shine heard the noise of metal being ripped. He looked up. It was the steel cab roof being torn off. The tornado rolled it back the way a key rolls back the top of a sardine can, then snapped it off and carried it away. Shine expected to be sucked up into the funnel of the tornado, too. But just then it got light. To his great joy, the train had shot right through the twister. Ahead was a peaceful country scene. He slowed down and stopped the train. Only then did he realize he was cut up, but the important thing was that he was alive and safe.

The tornado completely demolished the town of Griffin. Before the tornado brought disaster to that town it had two hundred buildings. After it left, only a few parts of four buildings were found to be standing. What had been a town was an area covered with boards, broken glass, and pieces of metal. To make things worse, a fire swept through the debris. Fanned by a wind, flames raced through the wood. Rescue workers tried to uncover and help as many who had been buried in the wreckage as possible, but several died in the flames. Out of a population of four hundred, fifty were left dead and two hundred injured.

No storm can last forever, and the great tornado of 1925 was no exception. It disappeared. But in its short lifetime, it killed hundreds of people in twenty-three cities and towns, making it by far the most violent single tornado in American history.

7. Xenia, Ohio — April 3, 1974

Every now and then cold fronts and warm fronts moving over the Midwest array themselves in such a way that the only likely outcome of a violent meeting between them will be a series of violent tornados. Just such conditions occurred on April 2, 1974. Allen Pearson, head of the National Severe Storms Forecast Systems, noted that a mass of exceptionally cold, dry air lay over Wyoming. To the south a warm air mass containing huge amounts of moisture was racing northward. To complicate and worsen things the jet stream, moving sixty-five thousand feet above sea level, was headed east-southeast. That was going to add to the fury of the coming impact. Pearson, who had years of experience behind him, knew that something big was going to happen. Looking at a map of the midwest, the only question in his mind was where?

The cold front moved southward into the Mississippi Valley during the night. Thousands of messages were coming into weather stations, to the National Weather Services, and to the

National Severe Storms Forecast Systems headquarters in Kansas City. Each message told of worsening conditions. Many meteorologists knew that they were watching a once-in-a-life-time weather situation. The worst day for tornadoes since March 18, 1925, was definitely shaping up.

Early Wednesday, April 3, 1974, warnings were sent through all the media telling Americans that tornado watches were posted for large areas in southern Illinois, northern Kentucky, and southwestern Ohio. At 8:15 A.M. Lubbock, Texas, radar picked up a hook-shaped cloud pattern. This is an almost sure sign that a tornado is brewing.

From then on, there were warnings. At 2:35 P.M. the National Severe Storms Forecast Center issued tornado watch Number 98 for a strip of land seventy miles on either side of a line from Jackson, Tennessee to Covington, Kentucky, and from a point fifty miles south of Jackson to fifty miles north of Covington. Lying in the northwest corner of this territory is Xenia, Ohio.

Throughout the day, numerous tornadoes hit the American Midwest and the Canadian province of Ontario. No one knows how many tornadoes developed that day. Some plowed through cities. Others roamed isolated country and were never even recorded. Before the day was over, 310 people in twelve states and in Ontario would be dead.

To describe such widespread disaster would obviously be impossible. It is much better to focus on one tornado and its destruction. Typical of that day's killer tornadoes was the one that devastated Xenia, Ohio.

Xenia, then a city of about twenty-five thousand is located more or less in the middle of the southwestern quarter of Ohio, about forty-five miles north-northeast of Cincinnati. In all respects it was an average Midwestern town.

Though people in Xenia had heard of the tornado warnings, few, it seems, paid any attention to them. Most had heard them in times past, and nothing had ever happened. Then too, Xenia

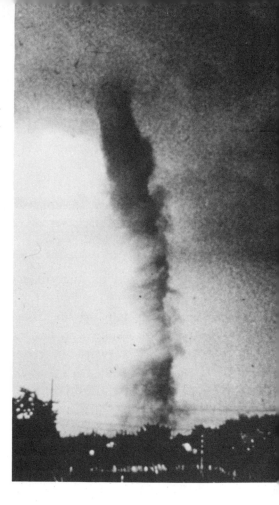

A tornado near Enid, Oklahoma, June 5, 1966. *National Oceanic and Atmospheric Administration*

was not in the center of the territory singled out for the tornado warnings. People carried on as they normally would. Children went to school, adults worked, housewives took care of babies. It was just another day in Xenia, Ohio. It is possible that not one person took the warnings seriously.

At 4:35 P.M. a tornado appeared southwest of Xenia. Because a few people say they saw two tornadoes at once, it is unclear how many there were—one or two. But those who say they saw two report that they merged and formed one large tornado. It was a huge one. The winds twirling around were said by some to sound like a thousand jet airplanes at once. Others said it sounded like a trillion bees buzzing in the air. It moved toward a Xenia residential district called Arrowhead. The tornado was so powerful that as it moved it simply jerked trees right out of the ground.

The first house hit belonged to Ken Shields and his wife, Pam. They were eating supper with their children. As they were talking, they heard the screen door begin banging. Annoyed at the sound, Ken went to shut it. As he did so, he looked to the southwest.

There it was—a huge cloud of roaring, whining, buzzing, twisting dirt. It spread over the ground like a loose sagging bag towering up into the sky. Black, ominous death was coming toward him. Oddly, Ken was more curious than frightened. He asked Pam, "Have you ever seen a tornado?"

She didn't bother to answer. She dove through the air to her children and pulled two of them to the floor. Ken, realizing the danger, grabbed another child and got under a sofa.

Then it hit. There was stupendous noise as the house exploded. Everywhere there was wind. But in seconds it was over. Ken lay on the floor. In his hand he held one of the legs of the sofa. The rest of the sofa had disappeared. He looked up. He was outdoors. There was no house left. He heard the children crying. He went to them and found them only scratched. Then he turned and looked at his wife. She was completely covered with blood from head to toe. From her neck stuck a piece of wood, but she was alive.

The tornado had come to Xenia.

The tornado moved at 40 miles per hour through the Arrowhead section. Buildings vanished in seconds. Trees were jerked out of the ground. Automobiles were sucked straight up into the funnel. Boards, flying glass, clothes, mattresses, furniture, kitchen sinks, flew here and there, cutting down people they hit. The trillion bees sang their eerie song.

One who died in those first few minutes was Eric Crabtree, a small baby. Diane, his mother, felt ill that day, so she had stayed home from work. The telephone rang. Someone informed her a tornado was on its way toward her house. She took the baby in her arms and held him. As the winds hit, she fainted. Then she came to again. She saw the walls collapsing and heard the wind ripping the nails out of the studs. The nails screamed. Above her the roof got sucked away. As she watched, she passed out again. The tornado pulled Eric from her arms to his death. So little remained of him that his father had to identify him by means of his clothes.

Most people downtown had no idea at all that a tornado was in town. They did not have any inkling that they were in extreme danger. Very few who saw the tornado telephoned friends or family downtown. So life there went on as usual: People stood in lines at the bank. Others sipped root beer. Many were shopping. A few men and women drank afternoon cocktails in bars. Unknown to them, a few had only minutes to live.

As the tornado prowled through residential districts, it gobbled up more houses. At one place it wrenched all the trees out of an orchard.

Virgina Wells was taking a bath as the tornado approached her home. Perhaps she heard it coming. Perhaps not. At any rate, she stood up in the bath, wrapped a towel around her, and had just stepped out when death struck. The huge, impersonal tornado decapitated her.

Fourteen-year-old Prabahakar Dixit had come to America from his native India to study. His proud father had saved money for years so that this would be possible. He was just learning about American culture. Perhaps he had never heard of tornadoes. It is doubtful he ever knew what killed him. When the tornado struck his house, the house exploded. A flying board hit Dixit in the head and killed him instantly.

The tornado left an appalling scene of death and destruction behind it as it moved on. The dead lay scattered in the wreckage. Many of the wounded wandered about dazed and unattended. Some were pinned under beams, cars, trees. But in the other parts of Xenia, no one as yet knew of their terrible plight.

The great tornado moved on toward the center of town, its gray elephant trunk sucking up whatever it touched. The insatiable monster seemed to amble along as though out for a leisurely stroll.

Near the center of town, in the path of the tornado, lay water pipes, electrical communications installations, and the police's radio antenna. The tornado headed right for them. Water pipes were twisted into noodlelike shapes. Electrical wires were snarled as though a giant cat had played with them. The radio antenna was scrap iron. Within a few minutes the city was without water, electricity, or communication. The police had no way of telling the outside world what had happened. They could not direct police cars because they could not send radio messages to them. The same, of course, was true for the fire department. The city was paralyzed. The tornado burst sewer lines. Disease-carrying wastes spewed into the air and rained back down over large parts of the city. Stinking mess was added to general destruction. An evil genius deliberately guiding the tornado through the city could not have done a more hellish job.

In most disasters there is an element of good luck as well as bad. There was an occasion of good luck several miles away from Xenia at Patterson Air Force Base. Just before 5:00 P.M., air force officers spotted the tornado on their powerful, modern radar equipment. From their calculations they realized it was moving through the heart of Xenia. The commanding officer of the base immediately sent medical supplies, engineers, beds, and supplies of food and water to Xenia. Shortly after sunset, even before Xenia could make its plight known, a long convoy of trucks was headed for the city.

At about the same time other rescue groups were receiving

first news of the disaster. One was the famous Box 21 Rescue Unit in Dayton, which had already won international recognition for previous rescue work. Its chief, Ted Howell, was on a highway when he heard of the disaster on his car radio. He immediately made a U turn in the middle of the road and sped back toward the stricken city.

The people of Xenia, who had not known the tornado was bearing down on them, were in their moment of greatest shock. The tornado may have split apart into as many as four separate tornadoes. Several witnesses report seeing four of them at one time. Others saw just one gigantic funnel of roaring wind that got stronger by the minute.

The tornado headed right toward the Arrowhead Elementary School. Fortunately, the teachers and children had left for the day. The tornado completely demolished the building. The gymnasium simply collapsed. Will Armstrong and his mother, Gloria Chambers, who were near the school, were dead in seconds.

Mike Kuhbander was eating supper with his two children. At 4:35 P.M. the telephone rang. His wife, Sheila, who worked at the Kennedy Korners Beauty Salon, told him a tornado was on its way. She told him to open the windows of the house. He did not really believe that a tornado could be nearby, but nevertheless walked about the house opening windows. Then he heard a sound unlike any he had ever heard in his life. Hundreds of nails being pulled loose from nearby houses sang an unforgettable song. For a split second he froze and listened. How eerie it sounded.

Then he quickly grabbed his children. He got them on the floor and then lay right on top of them, protecting them. For what seemed less than a second the inside of the house was filled with wind, flying objects, and dust. As quickly as it began, it was over. He stood up. Miraculously, the house was still standing. It was one of the few that survived a direct hit from the tornado. His daughter Kathy thought she was dreaming. She asked him to pinch her. Mike walked to the window to see where the tornado was going. His blood froze. The black twister was heading for the place where his wife worked.

The tornado moved relentlessly northeastward. It headed directly toward the Mallows' farm. For twenty years Ralph and John Mallow had been developing their orchard. The trees were just reaching their prime. The owners' long efforts would finally pay off in fruit and they would at last have a profit.

In minutes the twister changed all that. The dark monster roared through the orchard, plucking the trees right out of the ground like an angry child pulling up daisies. The trees shot straight up into the funnel. Many witnesses later said they were amazed to see hundreds of trees circulating about inside the twister.

On the killer went. It entered the outskirts of the business district. Simon Kenton School exploded as though it had had dynamite stored inside of it. Luckily, it was empty at the time. The cocktail lounge at Bon Air Motel slumped to the ground. Frischers hamburger stand became instant matchsticks. The Kroelher Manufacturing plant fell down like a house of cards. All the machinery inside was totally ruined. But amazingly enough, there were no casualties at all in the destruction of any of these businesses. In that sense, the city was lucky. Had children been in the school or workers in the manufacturing plant, the toll would have been horrendous.

The tornado marched to the very center of Xenia, toward an unusual encounter. It was about to be filmed with a movie camera. There are very few good still pictures of a tornado, and almost no movies. In addition to that, the tornado was about to be recorded on tape. For a tornado to be both filmed and recorded was unprecedented.

It came about because a Choctaw Indian, Thomas Yougen, had decided to tape-record the silence of Xenia. Yes—the silence. What a moment to choose. What irony. He turned on his tape recorder. As the tapes turned, Yougen heard distant thunder. He liked that. Somehow that added to the silence of the town itself. As he was thinking about that, he heard a new noise—a deep roar that came from not too far away. He knew immediately what it was. All his life he had heard of killer tornadoes. A tornado was out there!

Closer and closer the awful sound came. Yougen realized that he was in mortal danger and wisely ran for cover. Fortunately, he forgot to turn the tape recorder off. It soon picked up the sound of the Kroehlers plant falling in the wind. It was the first recording ever made of that sickening sound of nails being pulled out of wood as walls are torn apart. Then the machine went dead. By some miracle the tapes survived, holding a full record of the sounds of Xenia's tormentor.

As amazing as that was, there was another unusual event taking place. Sixteen-year-old Bruce Boyd had a movie camera in his hands. Though he had never used one before, he aimed it at the tornado and pulled the shutter release. The camera ground away, film reeled up and inside it. Silver chloride was capturing images of the tornado swaying back and forth in the sky. His mother yelled at him to run for cover. But Bruce, hypnotized by the scene, stood there and held the release back, recording images of houses bursting and trees being sucked up into the funnel. His frantic mother screamed at him to run for his life. But Bruce was too fascinated by the momentous scene. It is not every day that a sixteen-year-old gets a chance to record history. The tornado bore down on him. Only at the last minute did he dive for cover. He survived with his camera intact. He now had priceless film.

Six months later, NBC Television, in a special program on the tornado, showed Boyd's film. For the sound effects they used Yougen's tapes. It is without doubt the best record we have of a tornado. Viewers find it a chilling experience to watch the film and hear the tornado's deadly song.

The tornado plowed on through Xenia's downtown section.

Witnesses say that the tornado's funnel widened. Its already awesome powers grew in strength. In seconds it demolished Kennedy Korners, the gas station, the post office, and a supermarket. Several people were dead in a matter of seconds. Sheila Kuhbander, however, survived.

The twister moved into an older section of town where many of the houses were flimsy. David Graham and his wife, Sandy, were eating some snacks. They did not know that a tornado was bearing down on them. However, their son Bobby looked out the door and saw it. He let out a yell. The parents, realizing their danger, grabbed the children and ducked into their basement. But the tornado collapsed the house next to them, and when it fell, tons of timber, glass, and torn metal fell on top of the Grahams, trapping them in the basement.

At a nearby beauty salon and television repair shop, the owner saw the tornado coming. He grabbed everyone in the shop, including the beauticians, and pushed them into the bathroom. To protect the women, he lay on top of them. Though the tornado damaged the place, they all lived. The women had been so frightened, however, that their fingernails had taken much of the skin off the owner's back. The scars were still there years later.

The A & W Root Beer stand stood directly in the path of the tornado. As was usual at that hour, a group of people were gathered there. The employees were chatting and joking with each other. Not one of them realized that the huge tornado was plowing toward them. Betty Marshall, the manager, was overseeing the preparation of coleslaw and hamburgers for the next shift. Dorothy Rowland was in the back room. Diane Hall, the carhop, was out front. The radio was on and suddenly Dorothy heard the tornado warning. She went into the front room to ask the others what they knew about it. At that very moment, Betty saw it coming toward them. She saw the great swaying funnel smash Kroehlers into smithereens.

Betty herded the customers and employees between the ice machine and refrigerator. Because there was no more room, Dorothy lay down by the counter. Diane, who was outside, got into the car-hop room, which was in front of the building. No one had a chance to get properly settled down before the whole building went. In seconds the A & W Root Beer stand was in splinters.

Diane's fiance, Ricky Falis, was one of the first to run to the stand. Betty crawled out from under the pile of debris that had fallen on her. Dorothy had been dragged all the way across the floor. Her stomach was torn open. Diane was found crushed under a refrigerator. She was dead. Ricky went into hysterics. It took several policemen to hold him down.

The tornado cruised onward. A freight train going from Detroit to Cincinnati was just then rolling into town. The train's whistle blew. Its forty-seven cars rattled and bumped along behind it. Out of a sky as black as coal hung the swaying willowy trunk of the tornado. It looked so light and graceful. Looking at it, one could not imagine its destructive powers. But powerful it was. It reached down and picked up the rear cars of the train and flung them into the main street, blocking it. Those thousands of tons of steel meant nothing to the powerful tornado. It had picked up the train as easily as it had picked up chickens.

The tornado destroyed an old Xenian landmark, St. Brigid's Catholic Church. After standing proudly and tall for 123 years, it went in less than a second.

The tornado headed for the Xenia Hotel. For once, people did have warning. Knowing it was on its way, they scrambled downstairs and ran into the basement. While huddling there, they could hear the tornado approaching. The full force of the winds hit. The hotel shuddered. The wind screamed insanely. The noise sent shivers up their spines. Above all that, they could hear the destruction of the upper stories. Timbers snapped, nails screeched, glass exploded. The frightened huddle of people clung closer together. Then it was over. No one was hurt. Parts of the building had actually survived. The famous bedroom where President McKinley had once slept was spared. So was the bed he had slept in. But much of the hotel was gone.

Jack Jordan, editor of the *Gazette,* watched the funnel carry its cargo of giant trees swirling around and around. The trees rotated in the funnel as pieces of straw might in a whirlpool on a stream. It was a strange and profound sight that few people on earth have contemplated.

For a moment the sight held Jordan in fascination. Then he knew he had to move. People would be safer in the building's basement. He ran out on the sidewalk and told passersby to come inside. He herded them down the stairs into the basement. There was a large vault where secretaries were packed together like sardines. There was no room for him, so he huddled by a postage meter. As the tornado came close, his ears started popping. He looked at the vault. What if the wind slammed the door shut. How could those inside live? But the tornado moved away. They were spared.

The tornado marched into the oldest part of Xenia, the historical center. In it was the Galloway Log House, which had been there since the earliest settlers had come to the region. The logs went flying in all directions. And then the twister tore apart the Snediker Museum, the Moorehead House, and the Glossinger Center, all part of Xenia's past.

Detroit Street is one of Xenia's main thoroughfares. The tornado went right up the center of the street, ruining everything in its path. It demolished Central High School, which had been filled with students less than an hour before. It took the upper story off the Masonic Lodge. Then it tore off a wall from the library. Hardly a tree was left standing.

Its next target was Xenia High School. Here there were still students present. Several were hard at work rehearsing a play.

Drama director David Heath was guiding the students. A girl who was nearby waiting looked out the window and asked, "Has anyone ever seen a tornado?" Heath did not know whether to believe her. She said it so calmly that he wondered about it. He left his group of students, went to the window, and looked out. There it was, moving toward them. It was too late to do anything.

Heath backed away from the window. Students screamed. They could hear the wind. Above them steel girders whined and moaned. They twisted about as though they were alive. The whole roof was crashing down at them. Somehow Heath got the students into a hallway. There they heard the building going. In seconds they were all trapped. There were screams, sobs, and groans. Dangerous chemicals from a chemical laboratory above began to ooze down on them. In spite of all, they escaped. When workers later cleared away the debris, they found that two school buses had been blown into the building and were sitting on the stage where the students and Heath had been practicing moments earlier.

The tornado roared on as strong as ever. It killed Ruth Palmer in her bed. Ollie Grooms was crushed when a chimney fell on her. Clara Pagett, too was found dead. Linda McKibben and Richard Adams died at the Elbow Supper Club when that building exploded. Johnnie Mott was killed by a two-by-four spearing its way through the air. Clyde Hyatt was found dead.

Virginia McClellan did not like banks. Over the years she had placed money in a hiding place in her home. When the tornado destroyed the house, $1600 "safely" hidden there was suddenly gone with the wind.

Northeast of Xenia lies Central State University, which has mostly black students. Between the city and the university is open countryside, dotted with farms and homes. The tornado swept across that open land and headed right for the university campus. Its powers had not diminished a bit—in fact, its fury may have been greater than ever. As it moved across the open country it sucked more trees right up out of the ground and tossed houses aside. It moved on to the university, and plowed through the president's house. The president's wife probably never had even a second's warning before the whole house came down, killing her.

Nearby stood the brick post office. Inside was Oscar Robinson, who had been a postal worker there for years. The tornado was so powerful that after it hit the post office, there was not one brick left attached to another. They flew through the air like stone shrapnel. Robinson, caught in a literal hail of bricks, died instantly.

In each storm there are some freak occurrences. Logically, winds that had been able to toss railroad cars through the air should easily have toppled the Galloway Tower. The tornado smashed right into the old clock tower. For a second the tower was actually right in the funnel. People watching just knew that the structure was being torn apart. But when the tornado moved on, the tower was still standing, hardly damaged.

Tony Egwunyewga, a student at Central State University, came from Nigeria. Since tornadoes are virtually unknown in Africa, he had never heard of one. There was a track meet, and Egwunyewga was to run. He was standing on the track when a noise prompted him to turn around. There, swaying back and forth, he saw the black snake of a tornado. The trees were whirling around and around in it. He had no idea what this monster could be. Fortunately, the tornado did not strike the track meet, or hundreds more might have been dead.

Interestingly, Egwunyewga was to compete at another track meet several weeks later. Just before the pistol was fired, someone told him there was a tornado watch on. He was so paralyzed with fear that when the starting gun was fired and the other runners sped off, he held his position, frozen. People screamed at him to run, but he could not move. He was disqualified. He later explained that he could not get that terrible memory of the tornado out of his mind.

Another school right next to Central State is Wilberforce University. The tornado's howling winds smashed into it, too. Four buildings simply toppled over. A high tower fell and flattened the medical center. The force of the wind was unbelievable. When it snapped off the trunks of a row of old, large trees, they looked as though they had been neatly sawed off.

Because of the shape of the campus, the tornado's route once more passed onto Central State University grounds. The director of the credit union, Evelyn Rockhold, was in her car. Nearby the union itself flew apart as the tornado rammed it. Whole walls went flying through the air. Rockhold's car was crushed, and she died immediately.

Not far from the credit union stood a large stand of trees of great interest to botanists, ecologists, and other natural scientists. This was a piece of rare virgin forest, with a magnificent stand of beech trees. The tornado tore it to pieces. Not a tree was left standing. When biologist David Rubin surveyed the site, he was sure that the state, which only days before was going to declare it a "natural area," would sell it to subdividers. Odd as it may seem, the opposite happened. When botanists and other scientists saw what had happened they could hardly suppress their glee. They were delighted. Why? It was the first known virgin forest to have been destroyed by a tornado. All other virgin forests had been destroyed either by man or by fires. How, asked the scientists, does a virgin forest grow back? How would it grow back and be different from those destroyed by man? The state promptly preserved the area. For decades its regrowth will be monitored carefully by scientists.

By the time the tornado finished with Central State University and Wilberforce University, it had destroyed sixteen buildings. Many others were damaged.

As night fell, the administrators at Central State University saw that they had to act quickly. They had to find all the trapped people and aid the wounded. As they quickly got people together, they wondered why help was not forthcoming from Xenia. They did not know that all communications were down, that all the roads were blocked; nor did they know that Xenia itself had been so badly hit by the tornado. For years CSU had felt that Xenia purposely ignored the school because it was a black university. There had historically been friction between the university and the city, greatly magnified at times because of racial tensions. The next morning the people of Xenia were horrified to learn that the stricken blacks had had to go through the night without medical help, police assistance, emergency supplies, and all the rest. However, the blacks themselves did pull together to save lives and the university.

Walter Bowie was the assistant dean of students. The tornado came and went so fast that he hardly had time to realize what had happened. He automatically knew that he had to take charge. As he began to do so, someone noted his cut finger. Bowie looked down. Much of the finger was actually gone! But Bowie did not hesitate for a second, nor did he seek medical attention. He raced to his car and got a whistle. He blew it several times. Students and others from the campus gathered around him. He quickly organized a search party. He had the people surround the campus, forming a large human circle. Then they were all to move toward the center of the campus. As they did so, they were to search carefully for anyone who was wounded or trapped. The students found Rockhold and Robinson, but left their bodies (standard emergency procedure—leave the dead and help the living). Soon they began to find other people. A white man, Win Jackson, staggered out of a building with a badly cut black woman in his arms. A student ambulance picked up wounded coming from all directions.

After they had searched the campus, the students who were not hurt flocked to deep basements. There they would spend a miserable, terrifying night. They had no lights, no heat, no water, no sanitary facilities. Nevertheless, they stayed in the basements, for they heard on portable radios that more tornadoes were due.

It was not until 3:00 A.M that Xenia realized there was a disastrous situation at Central State University and at Wilberforce University. As though to make up for their earlier lack of attention, officials ordered help to be sent out at once to the stricken students. Air force trucks loaded with portable lights, mattresses, and drinking water wheeled northeast along the road—only to be blocked. Soldiers with chain saws and bulldozers were called up. The men sawed through one tree after another. Roofs, glass, steel girders, countless trees were removed with bulldozers and forklifts so that the trucks could move forward. Early in the morning the trucks finally arrived at the university. Lights went on. The medical corps took care of the wounded and carried the most seriously injured to hospitals in nearby towns.

Ever since the tornado had left Xenia, the townspeople were having their own problems. After the tornado had roared through the town with the sound of a thousand jet airplanes, a strange silence fell, a silence that bothered many people even more than the sound of the tornado. It was the silence of doom and death.

Odd as it may seem, the first sound heard in town may have been a laugh. Someone walking by a bar saw two drunks stagger out. They looked around. "What happened?" asked one upon seeing complete devastation everywhere. "Hell, I don't know," said the other, "but it wasn't like this when we went in."

Slowly people began to move. Some crawled up from basements to see that their homes were gone. Others stared at houses, which were cut so cleanly that they appeared to be sawed in half. Many noted the strong odor of wood, the wood of split trees and shattered timbers tossed through the air. Others noted the smell of sewage.

Then it started to rain. People heard the onset of the rain, and then the sound of screams and sobs. Children screamed incessantly. Others vomited. From under timbers and roofs came the cries of those who were trapped. Mingled in with those was the howling of dogs and cats.

Most people seemed in a trance. During the tornado they were so fearful that adrenalin surged into their bloodstreams. For a while they became superactive, but right afterward their bodies felt limp. An odd weariness overtook them. Some appeared to be paralyzed. This was because the adrenalin had overstimulated them, and they were now suffering from a form of shock.

At Main and Detroit streets people wandered about in bloody clothes with broken limbs and terrible open wounds. Some were actually bleeding to death. For a time others were too dazed, too much in a trance to give them any aid.

And then slowly people began to respond, to aid the wounded. The Graham family was still trapped in the basement of their house. Tons of wood, metal, and glass from the collapsed house next door blocked their escape. Water from a broken pipe was filling the basement. They would soon drown if they didn't get help. Passersby saw the Grahams' terrible predicament. With bare hands they pulled away the debris. David was rescued, only his legs injured. David and Billy, two of his children, were dead. Sherry was rescued too late, she was also dead. Bobby lay unconscious, water right up to his open mouth. But he was rescued alive. Sandy was the least hurt.

Other rescuers searching for the living left the dead for another time. The positions of the various bodies were marked while workers dug on, looking for others who could be saved.

Every now and then gunshots were heard—people shooting their wounded or trapped pets.

Many people imagined they had somehow become part of a television movie. The city looked like a movie set. It was very difficult to realize that the destruction and carnage they were looking at was real.

With 1297 buildings destroyed and 3300 others damaged, there were thousands of homeless people. They did not know what to do or where to go. Since all communications systems had been wrecked by the tornado, people could only find out what to do by word of mouth. Many walked aimlessly about in the pouring rain without any sense of purpose or direction. Before long, however, most people heard word of shelters. The largest was the YMCA. Though its gym was severely damaged, much of the building was in good condition. The frightened, the homeless, the injured come in. Nurses, who had no time to put on uniforms, began arriving from other towns. The upstairs part of the YMCA was turned into a hospital. By candlelight (there was no electricity) nurses cut glass, wood, and metal splinters out of people. They set bones. Because neither nurses nor doctors could be identified, keeping track of the total situation was impossible. Neither nurses nor doctors knew which wounded people had already received pain-killing injections, tetanus shots, or other medication. A few patients were in more danger from the chaos there than from the tornado.

And all the while more and more people were coming into the YMCA. If they were healthy, they were herded downstairs. But to get there, they had to pass by the bleeding patients. Quite a number of curious, wide-eyed children stopped to look. Seeing blood all over the patients and floor, some immediately vomited. A few became violently hysterical. In some cases it took volunteers and parents all the strength they had to quiet youngsters down. Delicate operations were being conducted by people who could not even prove they were doctors while wild screaming kids were running about bumping into them.

The people who made it downstairs fared no better. There were no lights, no electricity, no heat, no ventilation at all. The toilets did not work. The stench was horrible. Several who smelled it threw up.

Cots were brought in from nearby towns. A few people, utterly exhausted, lay down and slept like babies. Most tossed and turned. Few knew where their loved ones were. Many cried. Others silently stared at the darkness. But as bad as it was, almost every last person there was glad to be near living human beings. They at least had company, and lots of it. Quite a few people huddled together and talked all night. And how they talked. Some had a compulsive urge to tell others about their adventures in the tornado. Others spoke of fears for their families. As some unburdened their hearts, they became excited. Tensions rose. Some became completely hysterical. Fortunately, a large supply of phenobarbital arrived, for many had to be sedated.

Outside in the rainy night, other people were still suffering terribly. One was Ken Shields. As mentioned earlier he was one of the first to see the tornado. When it had passed, his wife, Pam, lay with a long wooden peg embedded in her neck. Ken gathered his children around and picked his wife up in his arms. He carried her to the car. Unknown to him, the tires had burst because of the extreme low pressure in the tornado. He roared off. The tires flapped about and came off the wheels. His wife struggled to take the wooden peg out of her neck. As he drove he had to stop her. He was afraid that if she succeeded, she would bleed to death from the resulting open wound.

He did not get far before he saw the street ahead blocked by fallen trees and parts of houses. He made a U turn. He went down another street. The same thing! More trees blocked him. He had to get Pam to a hospital. He was desperate.

A policeman stopped the car. He was going to tell Ken to stop driving around like that, but when he saw Pam he knew she might live only minutes. He quickly rounded up some men to move a tree from the road. Pam was put into the police car, which had its tires intact, and they all rushed to the hospital.

Pam was almost dead by the time they got there. Ken was sure she would not make it. As he waited, nurses noticed that his wrist was broken. He himself had not realized it until then.

As Ken was patched up, the peg was being safely removed from Pam's neck. Though she still carries a scar, she survived.

Xenia was badly damaged. It took days just to get such necessities as water, electricity, and food into the city. The death total was thirty-two. Though the suffering in Xenia was terrible it was only one of the many towns struck that day by tornadoes. Dozens of tornadoes did heavy damage, destroying $1 billion worth of property and killing 310 people.

8. The Killer Smog of Donora

October 29, 1948, was homecoming at the high school in Donora, Pennsylvania. The football team was scheduled to play. Preceding the game would be the annual homecoming–Halloween parade.

The events proceeded on schedule. Down Main Street came the majorettes. Their batons twirled; they high-stepped it, flashing smiles to the right and left. Behind them came the band. The homecoming queen rode in one of the largest convertibles in town. She was followed by spanking-new fire trucks, the pride of the fire department. They had been washed and the brass polished especially for this event.

But no one saw the parade—not really. The spectators who lined the street only saw shadows. They never saw the smiles of the majorettes. The homecoming queen was a vaguely glimpsed specter. The fire trucks did not shine or sparkle. For all the crowd could tell, they might as well have been painted battleship gray.

The homecoming football game was one of the strangest ever seen—or not seen, as it happened. Spectators who sat near the fifty-yard line could not see either goalpost. They did not see any touchdown. Players would occasionally move into sight, appearing out of a thick, horrid gloom of smoke, fog, and chemical substances that had mixed together to turn the day into a polluted twilight.

The smog made some players sick. They gagged or started coughing and could not stop. Some players spent a good part of the game on the bench because they became unwell in this foul atmosphere.

People who drove home from the game noticed a strange substance on the roads. Precipitating out of the thick, darkly opaque smog was a black tissue-paper-like clinging layer of some strange kind of soot. No one in Donora had ever seen its like before. The pavement was so black that as tires went over it, picking up the black gunk, they left light tracks on the road surface. Many people had great trouble even seeing the road. Familiar landmarks had disappeared. A few people wandered about lost for hours before they found their way home.

Fire Chief John Volk slowly drove one of his new fire trucks back to the firehouse. As he did, he silently prayed that there would be no fire that night. To begin with, the fire department would have trouble getting to the fire. When they arrived, they would not be able to see smoke coming out of a house or building. Searchlights would not penetrate this smog. He felt uneasy. This was the worst smog he had ever seen in Donora.

Smog was no stranger to Donora. In fact, thick smogs were rather common. This was in part due to the setting of the city. Donora was built along the Monongahela River where a deep valley made a hairpin curve. Any fog or smoke that got into the valley tended to linger. Because of the topography, it was difficult for the wind to blow it away.

At the time, Donora was an industrial center with a population of 12,300. In and near the city were huge factories. One of them was two blocks long. Tall chimneys were built to carry away chemicals, smoke, dust, and toxic gases, but naturally the discharge from these chimneys often settled in the valley. Thick smogs made up of smoke, water vapor, dusts, chemicals, and toxins frequently smothered the valley and Donora. It was not at all unusual to have smogs so thick that one could not see across the street.

Did the citizens complain? No. The factories represented progress and, most important, jobs. So what if you couldn't see down the block? So what if there were hillsides in town so poisoned with wastes that absolutely nothing grew on them? So what if you coughed a lot? So what if your eyes stung? Industry provided jobs. A man has to make a living, doesn't he? Who was going to complain when all the factories meant employment and paychecks?

Nineteen forty-eight was long before the first stringent federal clean-air standards were proposed. It was long before people were concerned about ecology—in 1948 nobody had ever heard the word *ecology*. It was long before people went on marches and held demonstrations about things like air pollution. No one would have dreamed of griping about the air being dirty, about a few black days in town. The people of Donora figured it was just a natural, expectable price to pay for economic security.

Ironically, it was Donora itself that would focus attention on air pollution. The town where air pollution was accepted as something to be expected would motivate the first efforts at setting clean-air standards. For unknown to people who tried to watch the football game that day, death was stalking the town. Death had arrived, shrouded in a black, silent, thick, toxic cloud that was becoming thicker and more poisonous by the hour.

A fog had moved into town on Tuesday, October 26. There was nothing at all unusual about that—fogs were a common occurrence in late autumn. The next day the fog thickened.

Smokestacks poured ashes, dust, chemicals, smoke, and toxins out into it. A darkening pall covered the city. People observed that this smog was thick, grimy, and smelled worse than usual.

By Friday, October 29, the smog was more than just different from any seen before; it was downright peculiar. People watched a freight train moving into the city. A thick plume of smoke came from its smokestack, but instead of rising upward and dissipating into the air as it should have, it drifted slowly down to the ground. Those observing were surprised to see smoke acting almost as though it were a thick black liquid. After sinking away from the train, it flowed across the ground. It was cohesive and substantive. Strange stuff.

People were beginning to remark that the smog smelled strange. Some said it tasted "rotten." Others called it "starchy." Still others mentioned "a sickening, sweet perfume." Though all agreed it was for the most part black, some mentioned that also to be seen in it were chemicals that were "scummy and white." A few said the sooty precipitate felt like grease.

All day the gloom thickened. By nightfall the city was lost in it. Everything was a diffused blackness. The lights of homes seemed swallowed up in it, as did the neon lights from bars and cafés, the street lights, and the stoplights. A cavernous gloom covered Donora.

Fire Chief Volk was about to call it a day at the firehouse when the telephone rang. He froze. A fire! He picked up the telephone. The man on the other end could hardly talk. He was choking to death, he said. He needed oxygen immediately. He was sure he would die. "Please help me!" Volk was stunned. He was not a doctor. He was not supposed to go running around giving oxygen to people. He asked the man if he had contacted a doctor. The man wheezed and sputtered, explaining with extreme difficulty that all the telephone lines to doctors' offices were busy. "Please, for God's sake, help me."

It was probably Volk who first realized that a crisis was taking place in Donora. A man was dying out there in the smog. And all the doctors' lines were tied up. Why? It was obvious. Others were also sick and in need of urgent help. Volk realized the situation. Well, he was not going to let someone die on the streets. He drove the fire truck to the man. He found him near the telephone booth from which the call had come. He clamped an oxygen mask on the man's face. Soon the man was breathing pure oxygen. The man lived.

The fire truck went back to the firehouse. The telephone rang again. It was another request for oxygen. From then on it was nonstop all night. The telephone never ceased ringing. Volk and his men went out on the streets time and time again taking oxygen to stricken people. The night was so impenetrably black that many times a fireman had to walk in front of a fire truck to guide it through the streets.

Because of the great number of people they had to help that night, the fire department began to run out of oxygen. Volk got on the telephone and asked fire departments in nearby communities to bring more oxygen tanks to Donora. Luckily, this request was fulfilled. Fire trucks carrying the life-sustaining oxygen headed for Donora. The drivers of the trucks were astounded at the thick wall of black smog surrounding the city. Once in it, they could only inch their way to the Donora fire station. But, through their efforts, enough oxygen got to Donora to save many people that night.

The doctors had their hands full too. Early in the afternoon, a patient passed out on the stairs leading up to Dr. Koehler's office. He came up the stairs gasping for breath. There was a horrid rasping sound as he tried desperately to suck air into his lungs. The extra effort of trying to climb the stairs was just too much for him. He toppled backward. As he did so, he crashed into the bannister and tumbled downward, thumping along. Hearing the commotion, the doctor ran to the stairs and to the man. He held the man's head in his arms. Though he was a doctor and used to seeing people suffer, the sight of this man fighting for air unnerved him. He had the man lifted up the stairs and gave him a shot to relieve his agony.

From then on, it was utter chaos at the doctor's office. The telephone never ceased ringing. Dozens of stricken people came in off the street and fought their way up the stairs. Every doctor in Donora was deluged with calls, with patients, with emergencies. Some of the doctors were in poor health themselves and were gasping for breath. A few gave themselves shots. Others drank a jigger of whiskey every couple of hours.

A major emergency had hit Donora. Many of its citizens were close to death. The fire department could not keep up with all the requests for oxygen. The doctors were swamped. Some made house calls. All night they walked through the streets of Donora. They could not navigate their cars through the gloom—it was quicker to walk. As the night wore on, the dead-tired doctors, several of whom had lung problems themselves, increasingly suffered the effects of exhaustion.

Did the rest of Donora know what was going on? Not really. Bars were filled with workers who had been at the football game; some people sat home and watched television; others played their weekly poker game. How could they not know? There were several reasons. First, the smog was severely affecting only the elderly, the very young, and those people who had a history of lung trouble. Though fully one half of the population was ill that night, many thought they were the only ones who were sick. Most had no inkling of the silent epidemic around them. Also, the city's one radio station did not broadcast from Thursday to Monday. In addition, those who did see people suffer did not know others were also badly off. The news did not spread.

Things got progressively worse as the night wore on. Some people, desperate to get air, stoked basement furnaces until there was a big hot fire roaring. The flames sucked air into the furnaces. These people put their heads into the resultant draft and breathed in the air. To some extent this worked, and it may have saved some lives. On the other hand, the last thing the city needed was more furnaces adding their pollutants to the air.

For hours, many elderly or frail people lived on a thin line between life and death. Doctors withheld the name of the first person to die. Reports refer to him as Ivan Ceh. He started gagging. A strange white froth bubbled up out of his mouth. He could no longer speak. He gasped for air, arching his back in the struggle to breathe. His skin turned blue. His eyes bulged outward. At 1:30 A.M., Saturday, October 30, he died. He was the first.

There were several undertakers in town. One was Rudolph Schwera. His telephone rang. Ceh had died. Could he please come over and pick up the body? Of course, he could. It was his job. He and his helper got into the hearse. What a night! They could not see the road in front of them. For a while Schwera drove on the lefthand side of the road, peering out the window and following the curb. At other times, his helper held onto the fender and walked ahead as guide. It seemed to take forever to find the place where Ceh's body waited. Finally they placed Ceh in the hearse and drove back to the funeral home. Just as they arrived Mr. Schwera heard that there was another body to be picked up.

Another death in Donora? Schwera was puzzled. How strange. Very rarely were there two deaths in an evening. That just did not happen in a city the size of Donora. There was nothing to do but to go and pick up the body. When he got back to the funeral home again, Schwera could see from the look on his wife's face that someone else had died. It was unprecedented. Mr. Schwera was, no doubt, the first person in Donora to realize the mortal danger facing the city. This was no ordinary smog. It was a killer. Whatever was in that black, gunky air mass was killing people, and it was beginning to kill them right and left.

Other undertakers in the city were coming to the same conclusion.

In spite of the fact that nineteen people died that night, no alarm was sounded. The news did not spread like wildfire. Donorans did not know what was really happening. Before Saturday's dawn, only the doctors, the undertakers, and their helpers and families knew.

By mid-Saturday morning, however, news of the doctors' and undertakers' unusually harried night was becoming known to several people. A few leading citizens met to discuss what to do. The town's burgess (or mayor), August Chambon, who ran a moving business, was out of town. He arrived back in Donora at two o'clock. A note written by John Elco, a prominent citizen, awaited him. Would Chambon please go immediately to the Legion Hall? Chambon wondered why. The strange urgency of the note puzzled him. When he got to the Legion Hall he found a group of men waiting for him. They told him of the deaths, that more were likely. They informed him that the town's doctors, some of whom had been working thirty-six solid hours, were ready to drop from exhaustion.

Chambon was stunned. Sickness? Deaths? From the smog? But there was always smog. He never knew that people could die of it. People might cough and complain, but die? It was unreal.

Chambon immediately got to work. He set up a central community center, arranged for out-of-town doctors and an ambulance from another community. He put out a call for aid from all over the state. At the same time he tried to assess what was taking place in Donora. He talked to dozens and dozens of people. All gave him information and advice. Later he said he received everything but the truth that day.

As equipment arrived—the ambulance, doctors, oxygen, and other emergency needs—the smog thickened. It looked worse than ever. Sticky and gritty stuff was everywhere. The pale sunlight looked as though it had passed through dozens of panes of dirty, greasy windows.

At three o'clock the last person died. After that, people who had been gasping for breath began to breathe more easily. Chambon was amazed. Why? The smog, as anyone could see, was still absolutely terrible. It looked like nighttime in the city, even though it was only late afternoon.

The explanation is simple. Some factory owners, hearing of the deaths and realizing the dangers, had shut down their plants. Though the smog thickened, fewer toxic wastes were getting into it. Whatever in the air had been killing people was weakening.

By nightfall, the telephones in the doctors' offices had stopped ringing. The telephone in the emergency center was quiet. No one telephoned the fire department gasping for oxygen. Though people were breathing in soot, gunk, dust, and ashes, they were all right. The poisons were gone.

All Saturday night the smog thickened. By Sunday morning it was blacker than ever. On Sunday night radio announcer Walter Winchell told the world about the disaster at Donora, and for the first time, people heard about the stricken city. Most amazed of all were the Donorans. Most had no idea of what had happened. They could not believe it when they heard that twenty people had died there.

On Monday the smog proved to have thickened even more. But this time, the air was damp. The smog mixed slowly with a wet fog, which turned to a fine mist, and soon there was a drizzle. Not too long afterward, a torrential rain poured down on the city. The rain washed down the roofs, the streets, the ground. The gunk, the scum, the gook, washed down the gutters and into the river. By late afternoon the air was clear.

On Tuesday, November 2, the twenty Donorans who had died because of the smog were buried. Ironically, it was a beautiful day. The sky was as crisp and blue and clean as only a sky in November can be. Trees were in full color, flaming red and gold. A cool, clean wind swept across the cemetery where the coffins lay.

The disaster in Donora took the country by surprise. Though there had actually been similar disasters, such as the one in the Meuse Valley in Belgium in 1930, none had previously occurred in the United States. Right after it, teams of experts poured into Donora to find out what had gone wrong. There were chemists, doctors, a veterinarian, meteorologists, statisticians, sociologists, engineers, a dentist, and others. Few disasters have been as thoroughly studied as the one in Donora.

The findings, however, were not conclusive. No one could pinpoint a particular chemical that caused the deaths. In spite of the fact that twenty people died and over six thousand were felled by something in the smog, no one knows to this day what it was. Most chemists think it was the overload of many different chemicals at once: sulfur compounds such as sulfur dioxide and sulphuric acid, fluorides, nitrogen dioxide and other nitrites, cadmium oxide, and other deleterious chemicals. Many of these, it is thought, combined in the air to form other, more complex, toxic chemicals. But after extensive investigations, after dozens of reports many hundreds of pages long, it all more or less remains a mystery.

One particular finding was exceptionally frightening. It was discovered that if the smog at its worst in terms of poisonous qualities (whatever they might have been) had lingered only a few hours more, most of the plants, animals, and human beings in Donora would have died. If the smog had been just a little bit more poisonous, the same thing would have happened. Few would have lived.

One might consider a disaster in which only twenty people died unimportant, especially compared to disasters where hundreds, even thousands die. Any such evaluation is misguided. The Donora tragedy, more than most, is an example of a terrible threat that potentially faces all of us who live in urban areas. Many American cities, including particularly such major metropolitan areas as Detroit, Los Angeles, New York City, and St. Louis, have large factories in them that can pollute the air to a point where deaths will occur. It is possible that, under the "right" circumstances, a killer smog will develop again somewhere and take a tremendous toll in human lives. This is especially true as more and more exotic and strange chemicals are produced. Donora may prove to have been a harbinger of things to come. Let's hope not. Perhaps through stringent air-quality controls we can avoid another Donora disaster.

9. Fog Shrouds the *Andrea Doria*

It is difficult to associate fog with anything harmful. All of us have enjoyed foggy days. Fog is so soft, so delicate, so silken that it does not seem possible that it can be dangerous. Yet it can be a killer.

For ships and airplanes, fog is the number-one killer in terms of weather. Odd as it may seem, more ships have been lost because of fog than from all the hurricanes, storms, and icebergs put together. Airplanes can easily survive lightning storms, hail, and hurricanes, but hundreds have crashed in dense fogs.

Fogs are like low-lying clouds. They are formed when warm air carrying moisture is cooled. As it cools, the moisture, which at first is unseen water vapor, condenses into tiny droplets of water, which are seen as fog. Sea fogs are usually at their worst near places where warm currents run close to cold currents. One of the foggiest places on earth is off the New York, New England, and eastern Canadian seacoast. Air moving northward first crosses the nearby Gulf Stream, which carries warm waters. This warmed air, slowly moving northward, has in it a great deal of moisture. As the air passes over the cold ocean currents near New England and Canada, the moisture condenses into tiny drops of water. These drops are so small that they remain suspended in the air. The fog particles, varying from about $\frac{1}{2500}$ to $\frac{1}{250}$ inch across, are held suspended by both the friction of the air and by the motion of the molecules in the air. They can hang in the air for days, even weeks at a time.

One might think at first that the only ships to have crashed into each other and sunk were those that lacked radar and other modern detection equipment. But are radar and other sophisticated equipment safeguards against ships colliding in fog? Not always. Let us consider two large ships, the *Andrea Doria* and the *Stockholm,* each of which had all the modern equipment anyone could possibly hope for.

On June 16, 1951, the *Andrea Doria,* the pride of the Italian merchant marine, slid down the ways in a Genoa, Italy, shipyard. The 29,082-ton ship glided majestically across the water. Thousands of people, from muscular, tattooed shipyard workers to dignitaries, cheered. It was by any standard a beautiful, streamlined, modern ship. It was Italy's best and largest passenger liner, a ship lover's dream come true, with perfect lines and beautiful proportions. In every way it had class. In terms of safety equipment it could not be equaled. Indeed, because of its many watertight compartments and the internal communication system that governed them, it was considered virtually unsinkable. Moreover, it carried two complete and separate radar stations. If one broke down, the other could function independently. There was also a complete and up-to-date meteorological station on board. The ship's radios could easily keep in touch with ground stations and other ships at sea. The *Andrea Doria* had sixteen aluminum lifeboats, which could comfortably carry two thousand people. Since only eighteen hundred people at the most would ever be aboard, there was a larger-than-needed safety factor. The ship also had very advanced fire-fighting equipment. It actually had a fire department. Its cabins were insulated from the hull. This meant that if there was a fire on board and the hull got extraordinarily hot, transmitted heat could not set fires in cabins touching the hull. For a passenger liner, the *Andrea Doria* was considered by all to be the very epitome of safety.

The ship was specifically built and designed for the Atlantic run between Genoa, Italy, and New York City. Almost without incident, the *Andrea Doria* easily crossed the Atlantic exactly one hundred times with complete safety and comfort. Its record was well known among knowledgeable travelers. Many sophisticated tourists, vacationers, and businessmen preferred it to any other ship on the Atlantic run.

On July 17, 1956, the *Andrea Doria* left Genoa on its hundred and first voyage. Captain Piero Calamai, who had been with the ship from the beginning, commanded it. After making a few calls at Mediterranean ports, the ship, carrying 1706 passengers, sailed smoothly out into the blue Atlantic Ocean, old familiar territory. Until 3:00 P.M. Wednesday, July 25, 1956, the voyage was uneventful. The well-trained, hand-picked crew did its routine job with elan and efficiency. The passengers enjoyed themselves, lounging by swimming pools, watching movies, working out in gyms, gossiping and clustering at the bars, dancing at night, finding romance and friends.

Captain Piero Calamai, noted for his confidence and almost aristocratic bearing, feared nothing—except fog. He issued a standing order concerning fog conditions. The moment that officers realized the ship was heading into fog, he was immediately to be called to the bridge, night or day. The captain did not need to be called the afternoon of July 25. From his many years at sea, he had a feeling that the ship was heading into fog and so he was already on the bridge. The sky had a suspicious hazy look to it. At 3:00 P.M., the captain saw the fogbank ahead. It lay where Atlantic fogbanks often lay at that time of the year, several miles south of Nantucket Island.

The ship was headed 267 degrees (almost due west) toward the Nantucket lightship. Calamai ordered a seaman forward to the bow of the ship to serve as a lookout and ordered the ship slowed down from 23 knots to 21.8 knots. More men were ordered to the engine room. To control such a heavy and powerful ship, it required many men just to turn the engine valves. Several steel doors were shut and bolted. These effectively divided the internal parts of the ship into separate watertight compartments. The two separate radar screens were being watched by experts. The green lines on the screens went around and around. Blips showed ships in the far distance. Calamai, very cautious but supremely confident, stood on the bridge. He would guide his ship through another fogbank. How many had he gone through in his life at sea? Probably thousands. Never once had there been any trouble.

Slowing down a bit, the ship kept on course toward the Nantucket lightship, which would be passed closeby. The *Andrea Doria*'s huge whistles sent out blasts of sound that were heard for miles around. They roared for a full six seconds every minute and forty seconds. They were so powerful that ships five miles away could easily hear them. The proud ship nosed its way into the gray nothingness of the fogbank.

The east–west sea lanes near Nantucket are divided. The sea lane nearest Nantucket Island is for westbound ships. To the south is a sea lane reserved for eastbound ships. The reason they are divided is, of course, for safety. Most of the sea lanes of the world are divided like that.

The *Andrea Doria* properly stayed in the northern sea lane. Several times the swift, sleek ship overtook and safely passed slower ships moving in the same direction. In each case the radar screens gave the navigators on the *Andrea Doria* ample warning. The men at the bow also made visual contact with most of the vessels.

Calamai left his post on the bridge only once. Just before supper, he went to his cabin to change into a dark uniform. For only a few minutes, he went to a bar and chatted with some passengers. He ate his supper, however, on the bridge. The fog made him a little nervous, as it always did. Still, he had every reason in the world to think the *Andrea Doria* would slip through the fog and be in New York City only a few minutes behind schedule.

As the ship neared the Nantucket lightship, the course was altered slightly so that the ship would not plow into it. The adjustment allowed the *Andrea Doria* to pass one mile to the south of it. This course, by the way, kept it well within the proper sea lane.

At 10:45 P.M. the radar picked up a pip. It was a ship, seventeen miles away and four degrees off the starboard (right) bow. Curzio Franchini, the officer looking at the radar pip, noted that the ship was coming toward them in the wrong sea lane. He told the captain that he thought it unusual for a ship to be in the wrong sea lane.

Captain Calamai replied, "Very unusual." The incident bothered him. He immediately asked the lookouts if they could make visual contact with the oncoming ship. They could not. Nothing. Just fog and gloom out there. Some officers went out on the open part of the bridge to see if they could do any better. Nothing.

Calamai told the man at the helm to alter the ship's course a bit more toward the south. That would give the other ship plenty of room to pass to the north of them.

The ships drew closer and closer together. Officers watched the radar screens. Seamen peered into the gloom and so did officers. The other ship was staying far enough to the north so that the two vessels would easily pass each other with room to spare.

But the captain felt strangely ill at ease. He went out on the bridge himself to peer into the foggy night. Nothing.

An officer remarked that it was very strange that they did not hear the foghorn of the other ship. Captain Calamai agreed. It was disturbing.

Closer and closer the ships came to each other. Radar showed that even though they were drawing closer to each other, they both had plenty of room—the other ship would safely pass them to the north.

Suddenly Captain Calamai saw the lights of the other ship ahead. It was less than a mile away. Now, ship's lights are arranged, by law thusly—on the left (port) side of a ship, there is a single bright red light; on the right (starboard) side there is a bright green light; on the bow, there is a white light; higher up, on the center of the mast, is another white light. If a ship is heading directly toward a person, he will see the two white lights, one directly above the other, and the red and green light on either side. If the ship turns, however, the person will no longer see the white lights, one directly above the other. In addition, he will see only one colored light, either the red or green.

Captain Calamai saw that the lower white light was somewhat to the right of the upper white light. This meant that the other ship was turning away from the *Andrea Doria* and would pass them on the north side. It was too close for comfort, but the ships would clear each other.

He was puzzled that the other ship was there at all. Then to his horror and astonishment he saw that the two white lights were again moving. This time they were moving into perfect alignment, one directly above the other. Calamai could not believe it. The other ship was bearing down on the *Andrea Doria* head-on.

Calamai had two choices. Standard procedure recommended that in case of an imminent collision a captain head his ship directly at the other one. In that case neither offered much area to hit. If they did, the bows were built to take a tremendous impact and still survive. But Calamai felt that he could dash ahead at the last minute with the *Andrea Doria* and avoid the collison altogether. He decided to make a dash for it. He ordered the ship turned away from the other ship. The helm pulled the wheel over. The *Andrea Doria* began to swing around, quickly changing direction.

Calamai's mind was spinning. Hadn't the other ship heard the foghorn? Why didn't it have its own foghorn blowing? It must have radar. All large ships did. The situation seemed impossible, like a bad dream. But he'd soon be out of the way of the other ship.

Then Calamai saw the two white lights change position as he swung his ship. The other ship was still coming toward him. Moreover, it was tracking him. There was nothing more that Calamai could do. For a moment he was paralyzed. Then he finally saw the other ship close in. He did not know what ship it was, but it was big and sleek, a passenger liner. He realized it was going to plow right into his beloved *Andrea Doria*. Calamai instinctively backed away from the railing just as the bow of the other ship began to tear into the *Andrea Doria*.

The ship cutting into the *Andrea Doria* was the *Stockholm*.

The *Stockholm,* the largest passenger ship ever built in Sweden, was the pride of the Swedish merchant marine. She weighed 12,396 tons and was 524 feet long. Though smaller than the *Andrea Doria,* she was just as beautiful, sleek, and modern.

The *Stockholm* had left its New York City pier at 11:31 A.M. with 534 passengers aboard. The vessel was headed east in the westbound lane. It must be stressed that there was no law that required the *Stockholm* to be in the other lane. When several countries had gotten together to sign an agreement about the shipping lanes just south of Nantucket, which were in international waters, Sweden had refused to sign the agreement. In other words, it was not illegal for the Swedish ship to be where it was. Captain Harry Gunmar Nordenson of the *Stockholm* did not feel any need to be in the usual lane. He had taken ships safely across the Atlantic Ocean 423 times, and he had often been in that lane.

For much of the evening the captain was on the bridge. But at 9:30 P.M., after a long day, he left the bridge in charge of twenty-six-year-old Third Mate Johan-Ernst Carstens-Johannsen. Also on the bridge were three seamen.

At 10:00 P.M. Carstens went into the chart room and saw a pip on the radar screen. He figured that the pip—a ship—was twelve miles from the *Stockholm* and to the south. When before long it was ten miles away, he realized it was a fast-moving ship.

Interestingly, though the *Andrea Doria* was inside a dense fogbank, the *Stockholm* was sailing under a starlit sky. This explains why the *Stockholm* never blasted its foghorn.

Carstens did not know that the other ship was in the fog. From his radar information he would never have believed that a ship in a fogbank would be moving so rapidly.

Carstens ordered twenty-year-old Seaman Ingemar Bjorkman out onto the outside of the bridge to search for the lights of the other ship. Awhile later, Bjorkman saw them to the left, or port. "Lights on port," he reported to Carstens. Carstens answered, "Okay."

Carstens left the radar screen and came onto the bridge for a good look. Through his binoculars he watched the lights of the approaching ship. He was certain all would go well, that the ships would pass safely left side to left side. (This was different from what the people on the *Andrea Doria* felt was happening. Even a subsequent long court case was unable to determine what happened. It is still not clear which ship was correct.) To give the two ships even more room, Carstens ordered the *Stockholm* turned more to the right (starboard).

A moment later, both Carstens and Bjorkman saw the other

ship turn toward them. Neither could believe it. It was unreal. Up until that moment, Carstens had no idea what the other ship looked like. All he had seen were radar pips and lights. Then he saw that it was a gigantic passenger liner more than twice as large as the *Stockholm*. He immediately knew that the *Stockholm* would slice right into its side.

Carstens reacted instantly. He telegraphed the engine room to go full speed astern. The men in the engine room had no idea what was happening above. But they knew that an order to reverse engines at full speed was only given on the high seas when a collision was imminent. They leaped to their posts. Frantically they turned valves. It is extremely difficult even to stop the engines of a heavy ship, and they had to be stopped before they could be put into reverse. Working as hard as they could and fearful of a crash at any second, the engine room men worked like demons.

Captain Nordenson, who was asleep in his cabin, heard the order to the engine room, for the communications system was such that all messages went through his cabin, where he could keep tabs on all that was going on. Knowing that the ship was in extreme danger, he raced to the bridge.

Nothing on earth could stop the *Stockholm* in time. The captain was still running up the stairs as Carstens and the other three men on the bridge in amazement watched the high bow of their ship take aim at the right side of the *Andrea Doria*. Right in front of the *Stockholm*'s bow were the lights of the *Andrea Doria*'s passenger cabins.

As the *Stockholm* plowed into the *Andrea Doria* the steel screamed. It was torn, bent, peeled away. Thousands of bright white and orange sparks, in a display of light bigger than most fireworks, leaped and fountained into the night. Hundreds of pounds of steel instantly melted. In a horrible way, it was beautiful. The 12,396 tons of the *Stockholm* kept pushing, pushing, pushing into the *Andrea Doria*. As it went in, it sliced, cut, and shattered steel and wood. After cutting thirty feet directly into the *Andrea Doria,* the *Stockholm* finally stopped. It had plowed into the *Andrea Doria* right below that ship's wheelhouse. The hole it made was in the shape of an equilateral triangle with each side about forty feet long.

The engines, at long last in reverse, slowly pulled the *Stockholm* back out of the *Andrea Doria.* But the forward motion of the *Andrea Doria* caused the *Stockholm's* retreating bow to bang against the *Andrea Doria,* breaking deck railings and causing other damage. Because of the collision, thirty feet of the *Stockholm's* bow was gone.

During the collision many died almost instantaneously. Dozens who died probably never knew what happened. Those who were asleep in their cabins never woke up. They went from sleep to death without any interruption.

There were fewer deaths on the *Stockholm* than on the *Andrea Doria.* The bow space on the *Stockholm* was the forecastle. Workers and ordinary seamen had their quarters there. Fortunately for most of them, who were stewards, cook's helpers, and kitchen workers, they had been called upon to do overtime work. However, four seamen were killed outright.

Another seaman was hopelessly trapped in the *Stockholm's* anchor chain. It snapped and started coiling around him as it plunged into the sea. He tried to fight his way out of the chain, screaming as it dragged him along. But it was to no avail. He was pulled into the sea and drowned.

Water flooded into the forward parts of the *Stockholm.* Captain Nordenson, who had quickly reached the bridge, worked with the other officers, who had also rushed to their posts. He ordered that water be pumped out of the forward parts of the ship and, at the same time, pumped *into* the rear parts of the ship. He felt that if the rear of the ship became heavy enough, the bow would rise up out of the water. For a while the bow of the *Stockholm* sank. The captain and officers feared for the worst. At any moment, a runaway flood in the forward part of the ship could take the *Stockholm* to the bottom of the ocean. Fortunately, the rear of the ship became heavier and began to sink lower into the water. Slowly the bow began to rise. Once the bow was up, crewmen shut forward watertight doors to seal off the forward sections. The *Stockholm* was saved. After the bow was later repaired, the ship remained in service for many years to come.

As the pumping was going on, an officer asked Seaman Bernabe Polance Garcia to go to the bow area and make a report on the damage. It was pitch black there, an extremely dangerous place to be. Everywhere razor-sharp pieces of torn metal that could cut a man to bits stuck up. At Garcia's feet were weakened plates of metal that could give way at any second, plunging him into a deep, dark opening below, where he would be cut and trapped by more jagged metal. Or he might plunge into the ocean.

Very carefully Garcia worked his way forward, taking note of the damaged areas so that he could make his report. Suddenly he heard a female voice cry out, "Madre. Madre." Garcia froze stiff. He was astounded. To begin with, he was positive that there were no Spanish-speaking passengers on board. Yet here was a voice crying out in Spanish for her mother. Second, what would she be doing up there on the bow, so far from the passenger areas? It made no sense at all. He could not believe what he heard. Then a sense of compassion overcame him. He called out in Spanish that he was coming to help her.

Slowly he made his way through a maze of curved, scythelike points of steel to a sight that astonished him even more. In the darkness, he could just make out a mattress from a bed. What was a mattress doing there? He worked his way to it. On the mattress lay a fourteen-year-old girl. No sheet. No blankets. Her yellow pajamas, embroidered with Chinese figures, was cut to ribbons. He stared down at her in disbelief. He reached down in the darkness and checked her for injuries. He realized immediately that her arm was broken. He was sure she also had internal injuries. Slowly, gently, he lifted her up in his arms and began to carry her back toward the midsection of the ship. Somehow he safely made his way back through the jungle of torn steel. All the time, he tried to calm the girl.

The girl's name was Linda Morgan, and her mother was Spanish. A few moments before, she had been asleep on the *Andrea Doria*. When the *Stockholm's* bow crashed through the walls of her cabin, it completely destroyed her bed. In pulling back, it gently rose on a wave and lifted Linda, on her mattress, away from the *Andrea Doria*.

Linda had awakened to see above her the black night and a moon. In the distance, no doubt from the *Andrea Doria,* she heard a woman sobbing. She thought it was her mother. She called out. Nothing happened. She stared at the sky. Her situation made absolutely no sense to her. She felt no pain from her broken arm. All she felt was a puzzlement. How could she be on deck under the open sky? She had no idea.

Slowly the pain came. She began to think that she was having a nightmare. But that made no sense either. This was not a bad dream. It could not be one. A sense of utter horror filled her. She screamed, "Madre. Madre." And that was when Garcia heard her.

Garcia finally got her to the midsection of the ship. In the lights he could see her better. She stared up at him, saying nothing but feeling a thankfulness for this stranger. Garcia carried her directly to the ship's hospital. Before medical help was given to her, she spoke to the ship's purser, Curt Dawe. He asked her her name. She told him.

Dawe was puzzled for he knew that no one named Linda Morgan was on board the *Stockholm*. When the girl gave him her mother's name, Jane Cianfarra, Dawe was even more perplexed. He doublechecked his records. There was no Morgan and no Cianfarra on the *Stockholm*. For an awkward moment there was dead silence. Dawe decided to try another tack; he asked her where she had come from.

She told him that she had come from Madrid.

Dawe still could not understand. Madrid? The ship had left New York only a few hours ago. What was all this about Madrid? He was trying to think of what else to ask her.

Just then Linda began to sob. "Isn't this the *Andrea Doria?*"

From all accounts, Dawe's face went white. His lips began to tremble. He could not even talk for a few moments. Slowly and sympathetically he told her that she was on the *Stockholm*.

Linda, of course, had never heard of the *Stockholm*. She had no idea that there had been a collision. She became hysterical. This had to be the *Andrea Doria*. She screamed and screamed for her mother.

Profoundly touched by the plight of the poor girl, the people in the room tried to comfort her. They checked her for internal injuries, but found none. They set her broken arm in a cast. They also explained to her how she had gotten onto the *Stockholm*.

Garcia figured that the girl had been in a cabin with her family and that no one else in the family could have survived the crash. He went to the captain and asked if he could adopt the girl. The captain told him he would have to wait until distant relatives were contacted.

At that moment, Linda's sister was dead, but her mother and stepfather were alive on the *Andrea Doria*. Her mother was trapped in a tangle of metal. Her stepfather was writhing on the floor of the cabin, so badly mangled that he wanted to die. He told his wife of his terrible pain, but she could not go to him to comfort him. There was no hope for him; he soon died.

Not too far away, Colonel Walter Carlin was brushing his teeth when he heard a terrible crash as the ships collided. He had no idea what it was. A moment later he stared helplessly at his wife, who was lying in bed in a pool of blood. He was dumbfounded. He started to go toward her. All of a sudden the cabin opened up. The wall and floor disappeared, and the Colonel stared into an enormous hole several stories deep. Through it he could see the ocean. He stood there dazed, not comprehending anything. As though in slow motion his wife, fell down, down, into the waves to disappear forever.

The collision had ripped open a corridor nearby. A naked woman, her arm badly cut, staggered along it. Several people rushed to help her. But in her stupefied state, she simply walked into the opening. Even as hands reached out to her, she fell into the sea, never to be seen again.

The impact of the collision killed forty-one people outright on the *Andrea Doria*.

The *Andrea Doria* was built with watertight compartments below the lowest deck and cargo spaces. Under conditions of a normal amount of damage, these compartments could easily have kept the ship afloat. But the *Stockholm* had opened up a huge hole in the side of the *Andrea Doria* that went well above and below the water line. The collision had opened up to the sea compartments that were not watertight at all. Water rushed into those compartments. There was no way to seal them off. Almost immediately, the ship listed to its right.

After hearing several damage reports, Captain Calamai knew there was no way to save the *Andrea Doria*. It was only a matter of time before the ship went to the bottom of the ocean. As reports came in, it was clear that the damage was even more extensive than they had thought. Valves quite a way from the impact point were not working. Critical electrical cables were cut. Captain Calamai told the officers to prepare to abandon ship.

Within moments came a horrifying report. The ship was listing so badly that only eight of the sixteen lifeboats could be launched. The tilt of the ship made it virtually impossible to get the others into the water. Some officers and crew members had tried to budge them, but could not move them an inch. They were also fearful that if they launched those on the other side the water pouring into the *Andrea Doria* would suck them into the ship, killing people.

It was a grim moment. Calamai knew he had to make a hard decision. Under normal conditions, he should have told the passengers to abandon ship. But he knew that would only create a panic. A fight for space on the lifeboats could break out, and many would be drowned in the struggle. Even worse things could happen. He issued no warning to the passengers. He kept the fate of the ship secret from them. Instead, he told his radio operator to send out SOS signals.

The distress signals went out. The U.S. Coast Guard picked them up, but they could do nothing. None of their ships happened to be near the *Andrea Doria*. Moreover, helicopters could not find the ship in the dense fog. Some merchant ships did pick up the message. One was the *Cape Ann,* a small freighter that had only two lifeboats. Another was the navy transport, the *Pvt. William H. Thomas.* These two ships headed to the stricken ship, located at 40° 30′ North and 69° 53′ West, about forty-five miles almost due south of Nantucket Island.

Two hours to the east by cruising speed was the *Ile de France,* which was going to Europe. It had passed the *Andrea Doria* only hours before. It happened that the captain of the *Ile de France,* Baron Raoul de Beaudean, had been looking at the radar scope when the *Andrea Doria* passed the Nantucket lightship. As the pip of the *Andrea Doria* merged with that of the lightship, de Beaudean turned to his officers and jokingly remarked, "Why, the *Andrea Doria* just sank the lightship."

At 11:20 P.M. the radio operator on the *Ile de France* picked up the SOS from the *Andrea Doria*. De Beaudean was puzzled. What on earth could have happened to such a large ship? A ship the size of the *Andrea Doria* would take many, many hours to sink. The *Ile de France* was exactly at the line where according to international marine custom, it could continue on its way and ignore the SOS. De Beaudean knew that if he continued on his way no one could fault him for leaving a ship in distress. Besides that, if he went to the *Andrea Doria* and it turned out that other ships had rescued all the people, so that he had nothing to do at the site, he would probably be severely criticized.

The captain went out on the deck alone. He lit a cigarette and studied the thick fog. A ship was stricken. He realized that if he did not turn around and go back and people actually died, he would never forgive himself. He walked back to the bridge and ordered the *Ile de France* turned around. In a moment it was headed straight for the *Andrea Doria*.

As the *Ile de France* plowed through the fog-shrouded water of that dark night, the captain doubled all the watches. He knew it was risky to go through that fog. He realized how easy it would be to collide with a ship. Despite all this, he asked the engine room to increase speed. It would still take over two hours to get to the *Andrea Doria*. He radioed that he was on the way.

Things were grim on the *Andrea Doria*. Moment by moment tons of water were entering her. Slowly the right side of the ship was being pulled under water. The decks tilted more and more. The metal plates of the ship could hardly take the strain. They growled, squeaked, roared, and sometimes shuddered as they bent. Strange vibrations shook the ship. Frightened passengers and crew members listened nervously. At any moment a critical plate could pop and the ship would plummet to the bottom of the ocean, drowning everyone on board.

Below the decks of the *Andrea Doria* where the *Stockholm* had crushed in numerous cabins, two women were pinned in the wreckage. One was Martha Peterson; the other was Linda Morgan's mother, Jane Cianfarra. Mrs. Cianfarra was bleeding, and one of her legs was broken. Mrs. Peterson was in much worse shape. Her back was broken. She was paralyzed below the waist, and held captive by tons of steel.

Mrs. Cianfarra listened to her husband cry out in terrible pain until he died. She was certain that her two daughters, Joan Cianfarra and Linda Morgan, were dead. She was absolutely helpless. When her husband died just a few feet from her, she was not sure she wanted to live.

Dr. Thure Peterson at first could not figure out where his wife was. Their cabin had been wrecked by something. By what? How? He had no idea. He groped for his wife in the darkness. The whole cabin was so smashed and turned around that he could not find anything. Hearing the sobs of the women, he moved toward them. Finally he found Mrs. Cianfarra, then his own wife behind her. He realized that Mrs. Cianfarra was held in by a maze of steel that could probably be cut away with wire cutters and hacksaws. But his wife was trapped under massive steel beams. He said a few comforting words to his wife, then went for help.

As he left, he realized for the first time that he was naked. He found a curtain and wrapped it around himself. As he walked, he discovered he had been injured too. He limped badly. Nevertheless, he made his way up some stairs to the upper decks. He asked several people for help, but they all turned him down for one reason or another. Finally a waiter, Giovanni Rovelli, said he would help him.

Peterson and Rovelli returned to the cabin where the women were trapped. Though they tried everything they could think of, they could not free either woman. Peterson realized he needed more help. Leaving Rovelli with the women, he painfully went back up the stairs to obtain more aid. As he walked through the huge ship, he noted that it had tilted a great deal more. Before he got to the upper decks, it occurred to him that perhaps a heavy jack could be used to lift the steel beams from around his wife. He went to the captain and asked if the Coast Guard could send a jack in a helicopter. The captain informed him that that would be impossible. Did they have such a jack aboard? inquired Peterson. The captain was sure there was none available on the ship. All he could do was request one from the *Stockholm*. The *Stockholm,* however, had not sent any lifeboats over. The captain sent a doctor and some marine cadets with Peterson to see what they could do about the doctor's wife.

With a great deal of difficulty, the men were able to cut through the steel and wires holding Mrs. Cianfarra. They freed her and put her into a blanket. Several men carried her to the upper decks.

Mrs. Peterson was still trapped and no closer to freedom. She begged her husband to put her to sleep with morphine, then leave her to die. He refused. He tried to think of something else. By this time almost an hour had passed since the collision, and the *Andrea Doria* was sinking farther downward. It occurred to Peterson that perhaps one part of the wall could be cut if a hole were first chopped into it with a fire axe. He found a sailor who was willing to try to chop out the hole. But as the sailor chopped into the wall, debris kept falling on Mrs. Peterson. The pain was more than she could bear. They had to give that up.

The sailor was just as glad. He fled, for he was sure the ship would go completely beneath the waves momentarily. Peterson went to look for a jack from the *Stockholm.*

But no boats had come from the *Stockholm.* On the *Andrea Doria,* Captain Calamai was deeply concerned. If lifeboats did not come, he might lose hundreds of passengers and crew. An hour had already gone by since the collision. The *Stockholm* was nearby, but no other ship was in sight. Every minute thousands of gallons of water were pouring into his ship; at any minute it might roll over or plunge to the depths.

The delay on the *Stockholm* was because the captain and officers there had to be absolutely certain of the safety of their own ship before they could send lifeboats to the *Andrea Doria*. They had to consider the danger that their ship might sink while their lifeboats were away. It took them over an hour to check every possible contingency. They checked watertight doors, valves, electrical equipment, pumps, and so on. Finally they decided that the *Stockholm* was safe.

The crew began to lower lifeboats to go over to the *Andrea Doria* to pick up survivors. As they did so, there was a panic aboard the *Stockholm*. The passengers, seeing the lifeboats go down, thought their own ship was sinking. They screamed and ran to board the lifeboats. The captain turned on a public-address system and explained in detail what was happening. The passengers soon calmed down.

We often hear stories of shipwrecks in which women and children leave the stricken vessel first. In the case of the *Andrea Doria*, it was unfortunately quite the opposite. The first people to escape from the *Andrea Doria* in half-empty lifeboats were members of the crew. However, the bulk of the crew stayed to the last, helping and comforting passengers.

Just as the *Stockholm's* lifeboats began moving across the water, the *Ile de France* appeared, breaking through an exceptionally thick fog. The *Andrea Doria* now lay in a clearing, with fog near it.

The sight of the *Andrea Doria* utterly amazed de Beaudean. The tilt of the ship was so great that he felt it might roll over in front of his eyes. He ordered the *Ile de France* to go within four hundred yards of the *Andrea Doria* and then he ordered lifeboats to the stricken ship. With searchlights aimed at the *Andrea Doria*, he could see passengers. Worse, he could hear them screaming.

On board the *Andrea Doria*, it was a scene of terror. Many people had panicked and were screaming. Others were confessing their sins to the Catholic priests. Some were catatonic with despair. Very few felt that they would live to see the dawn.

Unknown to the people on board the *Andrea Doria*, their luck had changed for the better. Aside from those killed by the impact of the collision, only a few more were subsequently hurt or died. One child, for example, died when its hysterical parents threw it into a lifeboat. Others were injured falling into the sea.

With the *Stockholm's* lifeboats came the heavy jack that Peterson and Rovelli needed to free Mrs. Peterson. Rovelli was injured in getting the jack aboard, as it crashed against him. In spite of suffering an injury that would pain him for the rest of his life, Rovelli helped Peterson carry the heavy tool down seemingly endless flights of stairs.

They positioned the jack to raise the beams that held Mrs. Peterson. They found they did not have enough room to move the long jack handle. The two men were almost in despair. Time was racing by, and the ship was sure to sink at any minute. They cut away part of the cabin so that they could fit the handle in the jack and have room to turn it. Finally the powerful jack could begin to move the steel upward. In a minute, Mrs. Peterson would be free.

As the jack slowly turned, Rovelli noted that Mrs. Peterson's skin was cold. Peterson took her pulse. None. He opened her eyes. She was dead.

Peterson bowed his head. Rovelli suggested that they take the body on a lifeboat. Peterson saw no reason for doing so. He decided to leave his wife where she was. He took her rings and kissed her good-bye. The two men wearily climbed the stairs to the deck. Both were injured and it was a difficult, exhausting struggle to manage the stairs and get to the deck.

All through the rest of the night passengers and crew members of the *Andrea Doria* were transferred to other ships: the *Stockholm*, the *Ile de France*, the *Cape Ann*, the *Pvt. William H. Thomas*, the *Edward H. Allen*, and the tanker *Robert E. Hopkins*.

It was the largest rescue operation at sea in modern times.

All in all, it was one of the most successful, too. By just before dawn, the officers of the *Andrea Doria* were sure that everyone who was alive on the ship had been taken off it. All that were left on board were some of the dead. Supposedly included among those missing at sea was Linda Morgan. It seemed as though all that could be done was to wait nearby until the *Andrea Doria,* which had shown such amazing capacity to float so far, finally sank. The human drama seemed over. But it was not.

Unbelievably, there was still one more person aboard the *Andrea Doria.* It was Robert Hudson, who lay sound asleep in his cabin. Because of injuries he had sustained a few days before the collision, he was under heavy sedation. Doctors had told him to take the powerful medicines and get rest and lots of sleep. He had gone to bed early in the evening after taking the medicines and promptly fell asleep. He never heard the crashing, tearing sound of the collision. He never heard the scurry of feet outside his cabin, nor the screams of the panic-stricken passengers. He slept on.

When he woke up in the dark of early morning, he was alone in the huge ship. He had no clue that anything was wrong. He reached out to turn on the light. His hand found the switch. He flicked it. No light. He flicked it a couple of times. He thought the bulb had burned out or a fuse had blown. He decided to ask a steward for help. He swung his feet over the edge of the bunk. He stood up. He felt as though the floor were strangely slanted. He figured that the medicines were making him dizzy. He shook his head. He steadied himself. He took a cigarette lighter and lit it. By the flame he checked his clock—5:10 A.M. He looked around the cabin. Things had fallen down. He stared at things on the floor. It was not the medicine. He was not dizzy. Something was terribly wrong.

He went to the door to his cabin and opened it. He peered into the corridor. Dull amber emergency lights lit the long hallway. All over the floor there was seawater and oil. For eighteen years Hudson had been an able-bodied seaman. He stared at the water and oil. The ship was sinking. He looked at the walls, all tilted over. Not only was it sinking, but it could roll over at any moment.

He screamed, "Is anybody there!" His call echoed down the empty hall. The strange sound, so hollow and lonesome, sent a chill through him. No answer. No one. He waited. All he heard was the sound of water seeping into the hallway.

Hudson realized there was no sense in calling again. He knew very well that he was all alone on the ship. He knew everyone else had fled. His only hope was to get to a deck. If he was seen before the ship went down, maybe someone would pick him up. He started walking down the hall. A terrible pain shot through his body. For a moment in his fear, he had forgotten he was injured. But now the pain came back with a vengeance. He limped slowly along the hall. He was fearful of slipping and falling because of the oil. He figured that if he went down, he would not be able to get up again.

As he walked along the hall, panic began to build in him. Fortunately he had been at sea long enough to know that he had to steady his nerves. For a while he was lost in the confusing innards of the huge ship. He noted the numbers on doors and tried to figure out the arrangement of the cabins in relationship to the hallways. The close air was stale, heavy, and hot. Though dressed only in boxer shorts, Hudson was perspiring heavily. He found a stairway he felt must take him to the main deck. Painfully he climbed it. He came to a huge kitchen. When he had seen it before, it had been filled with waiters, chefs, cooks, helpers, and dishwashers. Now it was empty. A few pots hung at strange angles. The emptiness gave him a strange feeling.

He pulled himself up another stairway. He was so weak and pained that he could barely make it. It was torture to put one leg in front of the other. Eventually he made it to the open deck.

He saw the predawn sea around him. The very first light of day was in the sky. Yes, he had a fighting chance for life.

He moved to the stern of the ship. The railing was under water. He held on to a rope there. Everywhere there were ropes and nets passengers had used in their escape. The sun was just rising over the far horizon. He tried to position himself so as to be seen more easily. Just then a wave broke on the deck and pulled him into the sea. He was sure he'd drown. His hand touched a rope. It was part of a rope net. He dragged himself back on board.

Three hundred yards away he saw a lifeboat with people in it. "Help!" Hudson screamed.

A flashlight beam from the lifeboat searched the ship. The beam found him. It shone right into his eyes. They saw him. A surge of joy went through him. He waved and hollered. He waited for the boat to come to him. To his horror, he saw that the men did nothing at all. No one touched an oar.

To make matters worse, another wave, then another, and another, washed over the stern. Hudson was so weak and injured that each one knocked him down. He was battered and bruised and cut.

Hudson, in agony, alternately yelled and cursed the men in the lifeboat. More waves knocked him down.

Slowly Hudson realized that he would die. There was no hope for him. Abruptly he stopped cursing. He prayed to God either to save his life or his soul. He asked forgiveness of his sins and prepared himself for death.

Nevertheless, he called to the boat again and again. He started crying. He knew the men in the boat were afraid to come to him. They were afraid the ship would go down and catch the little lifeboat in the undertow, sucking it down into the sea. He wept. After a while he was weeping so badly that he did not notice the men begin rowing toward him. The boat sped across the water. The sailors rowing it were frightened.

Beautiful luxury liner the *Andrea Doria* sinks after its collision with the *Stockholm*. An empty lifeboat floats nearby. *Official U.S. Coast Guard Photo*

When they got to Hudson, they jerked him off the *Andrea Doria* as fast as they could, turned the lifeboat around, and rowed for their very lives. It was 7:30 A.M. The lifeboat took him to the *Robert E. Hopkins*. When he got aboard, an officer offered him a fifth of bourbon. Hudson drank every drop. Interestingly, after surgery and physical therapy, Hudson recovered fully and spent the rest of his life as a sailor.

At 10:09 A.M., July 26, 1956, the *Andrea Doria* finally plunged beneath the waves, going bow first. For a moment the stern stood up from the sea. The huge glistening propellers shone in the sunlight. As the ship sank it created an enormous whirlpool that rotated around and around for over fifteen minutes. The waters turned rainbow colors. The pride of the Italian shipyards rested at 225 feet below the waves of the Atlantic Ocean.

Some of the *Andrea Doria's* officers, now safe on rescue ships, openly wept when they saw their ship go under. For a while, as though stunned, the other ships stayed there. Then, realizing there was nothing more that could possibly be done, they headed for the coast to deliver the survivors to American ports.

The crippled *Stockholm* slowly headed for New York. Just as it got under way, a very large piece of metal from the *Andrea*

Doria fell from the bow. A woman passenger had been encased in it. The dead woman, loosened from the metal, slowly tumbled into the sea and was swept away.

Altogether forty-six died on the *Andrea Doria* and five died on the *Stockholm*. The wonder is that so many people on both the *Andrea Doria* and the *Stockholm* were rescued. Quick action with the *Stockholm's* pumps saved the ship from sinking with all aboard. The action of rescue ships saved most of the people on the *Andrea Doria*. It was, all in all, a story of a great rescue.

There was only one more drama to be played out.

On the *Stockholm* was Linda Morgan, now according to all official reports declared dead. In the confusion of the night, it had been impossible for officers on the *Stockholm* to explain she was alive on their ship.

Linda, in the ship's hospital, was convinced all her family was dead. Only one person could be alive, her father, Edward Morgan, a news broadcaster. Edward Morgan had actually gone on the air and reported news of the ships' collision to his radio audience. Concerned radio officials watched him nervously, for they knew it was possible his family had been killed. Morgan somehow carried the newscast off without a hint of difficulty.

Linda's mother, Jane Cianfarra, was on the *Ile de France*. When it came into New York Harbor with its unexpected cargo of refugees, ships greeted it with whistles, sirens, and horns. Edward Morgan raced aboard the *Ile de France* when it docked and met his ex-wife in the ship's hospital. She told him that Linda was dead, that she had probably fallen into the sea, for she had not been found aboard the *Andrea Doria*. Not only that, but Thure Peterson had reported seeing the bodies of both Joan and Linda.

Morgan telephoned Peterson and asked him directly if he had seen the bodies. Peterson said that he had.

Morgan felt dazed, but somehow he could not give up all hope. One by one the rescue ships docked. No Linda on any of them. The *Stockholm* moved at very slow speed toward New York City. A radio dispatcher on board mentioned Linda. The report of his radio announcement reached Edward Morgan.

Was it true? he wondered. Being an experienced newsman, he knew only too well how reports could get mixed up. Perhaps it was a mistake. Anyway, it seemed illogical that Linda really could have been on the *Stockholm*. That made no sense at all. Even so, was it true?

Edward Morgan went to the *Stockholm*. At first the officers would not let him on board. He flashed his press credentials at them. But they were for Washington, D.C., not for New York. There was no way he could get on board. Finally he talked with officials and explained his mission. There was a considerable delay. Was Morgan just trying to get a story? What was all this about anyway, wondered the officials. Finally they let him up the gangplank.

He bumped into Purser Curt Dawe. Before Morgan had a chance to open his mouth, Dawe told him that Linda had been an absolutely wonderful patient.

Edward Morgan stared at the man and studied his face. His heart beat faster and faster. He hardly dared believe it. It still made absolutely no sense. How could she possibly be on the *Stockholm?* It was too good to be true. He felt for a moment that there was a mistake of some sort. He was sure his hopes would soon be dashed. He had to be certain it was her—really her. He asked to see the girl. Could he go to the ship's hospital? he asked.

Dawe explained that Linda had been taken off the ship. She was in St. Vincent's Hospital. Edward Morgan raced down the gangplank and got a taxi.

At the desk of St. Vincent's Hospital, he asked to see Linda Morgan. After another battle with red tape, the hospital officials took him to a nurse. She led him down a long hallway. They went into a room. Edward Morgan quietly walked toward the bed and the girl lying in it. It was Linda. For a while he could not believe he was looking at his daughter. But it was his daughter! It was Linda! He rushed to her and threw his arms around her.

She asked about her mother and sister and stepfather. She was sure they were dead. Edward Morgan told her that her mother was alive. But, he sadly informed her, her sister and stepfather were dead. For a while they both cried together.

Later, Edward Morgan went to a pay telephone and called his wife. He told her to brace herself. Because she had seen the wreckage and what had happened, she had not believed that Linda could be alive, no matter what the rumors were. She tried to brace herself for the worst. Her ex-husband told her that it was true—their daughter was alive. Moreover, he had actually seen her, hugged her, and talked to her.

Jane Cianfarra was speechless with surprise. Her daughter was alive? How? She had seen it all: the wreckage, the cabin torn open. She had somehow landed on the *Stockholm* with only a broken arm? It was beyond belief, beyond any reason.

Edward Morgan, waiting on the other end of the line, heard sobs of happiness coming through the receiver.

Twenty-five years after the *Andrea Doria* sank, an interesting postscript was added to its story. Elga Anderson and her husband, Peter Gimbel, organized the *Andrea Doria* film expedition. It was their purpose to send divers down to search the sunken vessel and to report on the actual damage to it. During the month of August 1981, several dives were made to the ship. It was found lying on its side in about two hundred feet of water. Its paint had gone. In the murky water, it was difficult for divers to explore the ship. However, they did discover that the damage to the *Andrea Doria* was much worse than anyone had imagined. There was massive damage done to the generating room. The *Stockholm* had torn away so much of the ship that no watertight compartments could have saved the *Andrea Doria*.

The Anderson-Gimbel expedition had another purpose as well—recovery of two large safes on board. One belonged to the Bank of Rome and the other was the purser's safe. One of the safes was recovered from the ship and hoisted to the surface.

10. The Idaho Lightning Fire of 1910

During a period of drought, lightning is a major threat to forests. Many fires are started when lightning hits tall trees in a tinder-dry area, especially on ridges. It does not have to be raining for lightning to strike.

Thunderstorms, which generate lightning, are amazingly powerful. Most are formed when cold air masses meet warm air masses. The cold air sweeps under the warm air. As it does so, it rapidly shoves the warm, moist air to much higher elevations. As the warm air rises, it quickly cools, and whatever moisture is in it condenses. Quite often huge thunderclouds form, rising over four miles in height. Snow forms in the upper regions of such clouds. As it falls, it melts and turns to rain. In large, tall thunderclouds strong winds blow falling rain back up inside the cloud. The rain freezes and forms hail. And, of course, along with the thunderclouds come thunder and lightning.

Scientists know there are different circumstances under which lightning can be formed. So far they are not sure exactly how it is generated. They do know lightning has no necessary connection with rain, hail, or snow, except insofar as they are particles. Lightning is frequently generated inside hot, dry dust clouds produced during volcanic eruptions. Lightning has also been observed in windblown clouds of dust. Lightning can be formed so long as some sort of particles are in the air, and it makes no difference if they are dry or wet.

It is quite likely that many forest fires start because of dust-formed lightning. They may form when lightning jumps from a thundercloud to a dust cloud and then jumps to the dry trees, setting them on fire. Fires can also start even when rain from a thundercloud does not quite reach the ground, but rather evaporates in thin air, as it so often does in dry western states. Though the rain does not reach the ground, lightning from the cloud does, and a fire in dry trees begins.

Though scientists do not know exactly what causes lightning, two theories are widely held. Snow, ice, rain, or dust may capture and transport ions found in the atmosphere and sort them out. It may be that electrical charges are generated when two particles rub against each other. As they do, they wipe electrons off one particle and build them up on another.

Meteorologists know that thunderclouds have three layers of different charges in them. The top of a thundercloud has mostly positive charges. The middle has mostly negative charges. The base has mostly positive charges.

These charges are kept from immediate sparking, because air happens to be an excellent insulator. It is very difficult for a spark to jump through it. However, once the charges become powerful enough to overcome the insulating effect of the air, they do spark. Once the process starts, charges build up quickly in the cloud, and a bolt of lightning streaks through the air. Lightning often goes from one part of a cloud to another. Sometimes lightning will jump from one cloud to another cloud.

Naturally, we are most interested in lightning bolts that go from a cloud to the ground. Lightning goes from the positively charged base of a cloud to the negatively charged ground. Scientists are not sure if the ground is always negatively charged. Most think that it is not. Instead, the positively charged cloud overhead attracts negatively charged particles to move through the ground until they collect directly beneath it. When the charges become powerful enough to overcome the insulation of the air, the lightning strikes. The first stroke darts downward at about 90 miles per second. This downward stroke is made up of two parts. In the center of the stroke is a core about one half to one inch in diameter. The core carries the electrical charge. Surrounding the core is a sheath of electrically charged particles. This is mainly what we see when we see a lightning stroke.

When the core touches the ground, the electrical charges in the ground shoot right back up the core. What appears to our naked eye as one stroke is in reality two strokes; a down stroke almost instantaneously followed by a return stroke along the same path. Only exceptionally high-speed cameras, spectographic photographs, and the use of other modern equipment have revealed this sequence of events to us.

The electricity in the return stroke can be as low as 20,000 amperes or as high as 200,000 amperes. It can produce 30 million volts. A stroke, as we see it, can last from a tenth of a second to two seconds. The temperature of the stroke is about 30,000°F. Considering that iron *boils* at 4982°F, we can see that this is a tremendously hot temperature. The air around the stroke is heated so rapidly that it expands at supersonic speeds. This sudden expansion creates shock waves that rapidly decay into sound waves, which we then hear as thunder. Thunder can be so loud that it will be heard as far away as fifteen miles from its source.

Much of the energy from lightning is in the form of radio

waves. These can travel tremendous distances and cause static on radios. One thunderstorm in the tropics disturbed radios in Norway 3500 miles away.

Few mountain ranges anywhere are as rugged as the Bitterroot range bordering Idaho and Montana. Hundreds of jagged peaks stand high in the air. Canyons slice into the ranges. This is wild and desolate country. Travelers must hike or ride horses on twisting mountain paths. Even today there is less than one person per square mile living there.

In 1910 a few prospectors lived in the hills. They had constructed small cabins in clearings. During the day, while their heads were filled with dreams of riches, their hands became blistered from wielding picks and shovels. Others in the region were lumbermen, railroadmen, saloon keepers and a few homesteaders who owned farms here and there. The United States Forest Service of the Department of Agriculture had supervisors, rangers, and crews in the region. The forests, among the largest and most productive in the country, were under the direction and control of the Forest Service.

It was the duty of the foresters to spot and control any fires that might break out. During normal wet years there were few fires. In dry years there were more. To see what the fire hazards of 1910 might be, Elers Koch and a crew of men hiked into the heart of the mountains in April to check the snow depth. In the mountains the drifts were so firm and packed that the men could cross them without snowshoes. The crew measured the depth of the snow and reported that there was a normal amount in the mountains. The foresters were glad to hear that moisture levels were high. The year was off to a good start. Perhaps there would not be any serious fires.

But then weather conditions changed. Rainfall dropped off during the rest of the spring. The month of May was exceedingly dry. Parching winds soughed through the tall pines. Green

During a severe thunderstorm, a bolt of lightning streaks to the ground. *National Oceanic and Atmospheric Administration*

plants turned sickly. Brownish bare spots appeared on the hills. June was much hotter than usual. Snow fields that usually remained in the high country until July disappeared. Streams became mere trickles. A few fires broke out here and there, but crews easily controlled them.

By July, however, a dangerous situation was rapidly developing. A persistent, hot wind, dry as a bone, blew all month from the southwest. Plants withered. In late July, more fires broke out. Three thousand men were in the Bitterroots fighting them. Though they worked under extremely difficult conditions, they managed to keep the fires under control.

By August 1, an emergency situation existed. The forests were the driest on record. A call for help went out. President Taft ordered ten companies of U.S. Army troops into the region. A few very large fires started in the first week of August, but they were quickly contained and brought under control. But on August 10, the humidity dropped almost to zero. Whatever moisture there was in plants and the ground quickly evaporated. A hot wind sprang up and soon reached gale force. Leaves that had held moisture a few days before dried out totally, becoming paper thin and extremely flammable. Between August 10 and 12, a few clouds, which never released a drop of rain, hovered over the high peaks. Then lightning streaked down from the sky. Yellow bolt after yellow bolt hit the ridges, starting numerous fires.

On August 12, the winds became even stronger. The forest could take no more. Everywhere it exploded into flames. That date was forever termed "the day of the blowup." It was as though the whole forest ignited at once.

Within hours after the blowup the sky all through the region turned an eerie yellow. Such skies are only seen in the largest of forest fires. For many, it was as though the end of the world had come. The sky darkened in the afternoon as ashes and smoke filled the air. Soon the region was plunged into a premature twilight.

Still more lightning bolts shot down into the forest. More and more fires sprang to life. The wind hurled flaming branches, sparks, and embers through the air. They ignited everything they touched. Tall trees suddenly blazed forth almost explosively.

The situation was desperate. One of America's worst forest fires was raging. A whole region was threatened. To say it was out of control minimizes the force of the fire. Nothing on earth could have stopped it. Thousands of acres became sheets of towering, brilliant, yellow-white flames. Pushed by a fierce wind, they raced down the mountains toward cabins, roads, railroads, wooden railroad bridges, and towns.

Wallace, though a small railroad and lumberman's town, was the largest in the region. It was immediately threatened. People stood in the streets and looked at the towering columns of smoke in the distance. All were familiar with forest fires, but they realized they were witnessing a sight few people on earth had ever seen. One could hardly call it a forest fire. It was something of an entirely different magnitude.

It was up to Supervisor W. C. Weigle of the Forest Service to do something. When fire broke out, it was his job to try to stop it and to take care of the people in the region. Weigle, of course, realized that this fire was unstoppable. He told the officials of the Oregon-Washington Railway and Navigation Company to get two evacuation trains ready. All the people in Wallace were told to be prepared to leave on a moment's notice. Just before the trains were to depart, they would blow their whistles several times in succession. Then, by God, run for your life.

At four o'clock in the afternoon Weigle went up Canyon Creek to see whether the fire would be coming down it. He had not gone very far when he heard a noise he would never forget. It was the roaring of a great whirlwind. He turned around. The fire was coming over a hill and headed directly for Wallace. He raced back and warned the trains' engineers. The whistles blew loudly. Men, women, and children, carrying their possessions, climbed into the trains. The engineers gave their whistles one last long howl. No one else appeared. The steam went into the huge engine cylinders, and slowly the wheels began to turn.

Oddly enough, as the trains began to leave, two companies of U.S. Army troops marched into town. They stationed themselves and waited. They did not wait long. Tall flames bent in the wind shot down the hills. Cabins caught fire. The troops fought back with shovels, water, and wet gunny sacks. Soon they were not only battling for the town but for their lives. Then the wind carried the flames away. The troops had won a victory of sorts. Two-thirds of the town remained. But of the other one-third, all one could see were stone foundations, ashes, and broken glass.

The Wallace relief train headed for other towns where refugees waited. It stopped at Mullan, Saltese, Taft, De Borgia,

Haugan, and Tuscor. At each stop frightened people climbed aboard. All knew that the fire was not only moving closer but threatened the railroad itself. Already, behind them, the fire had burned away wooden railroad bridges. They had gone fast. Flames quickly leaped through the framework of the bridges. In minutes the rails on top twisted, then sagged and fell into the gullies below. At any moment the fire could halt the train and strand the passengers in the middle of an inferno.

As the people got on, they also knew they probably would never see these little towns again. They were correct. The towns were completely destroyed.

There was a tragic accident on one of the trains. One badly burned man who had been wrapped in bandages until he looked like a mummy was sitting in a dark, unlit car. A friend who came to see how he was doing lit a match to look at his burns. The match caught the bandages on fire. The poor man leaped from the car and ran screaming about in a field until he died.

Other trains on other lines not yet threatened by flames were also picking up refugees. It is estimated that over a thousand people from Avery to Taft Tunnel were saved from death by the trains. That this could be done was something of a miracle. Sixteen bridges along the trains' route were consumed in the flames, but only after the trains had passed. One was a very large bridge 775 feet long.

Dramas took place all through the Bitterroot Mountains. One occurred twelve miles south of Wallace. In the high country there, fifty men under the leadership of Ranger John W. Bell were fighting a fire, but the gale force winds quickly fanned it into a holocaust. Bell realized that the men were in immediate danger. The flames would reach them at any moment. Bell stopped the firefighters from working and led them to a nearby clearing that was a mere two acres in size. Bell hoped to get the men into a creek that ran through it.

The men raced through the forest, but they were not fast

Families, who have just fled from their homes, watch the smoke from a large forest fire in Idaho. *World Wide Photos/National Archives*

enough. The flames surrounded them. The men darted through the flames. Three who almost reached the clearing died when a tall burning tree fell on them. Seven men spotted a vegetable cellar owned by a settler. They got into it and shut the door. The rest of the men got into the creek itself. They wet themselves down and lay down in the shallow water.

The flames engulfed the clearing. One by one the men in the creek fainted from the heat. The seven in the cellar were roasted to death. When the fire moved on, only one man could walk. Bell ordered him to go to Wallace for help. The others waited in a burned-out hell. The air was filled with lingering smoke. Ashes rained down on them. Trees had been reduced to smoking charcoal stumps. The men who were badly burned wondered if their companion could actually make it to Wallace. It not, they would all surely die.

The man staggered on toward Wallace, limping through a nightmare world of blackened stumps, hot ashes, and still-burning trees. Each step was an agony, but he made it. In Wallace he gave officials the news about the men in the clearing. The route to the men was so difficult and dangerous that it took the rescue workers forty-eight hours of travel to get to the stricken men. As they literally chopped and hacked their way through the broken maze of burned trees, they could hardly believe that the messenger had ever accomplished his mission. The firefighters were found, and doctors in the relief party did what they could for them. Not one man could walk. The living were carried out on horses. The dead were buried in the clearing—the Reverand R. F. Carter officiated. Few burial services have ever been given in such a hellish-looking place.

All that day there were tragic occurrences. Some seeing the flames gave up all hope of escape. A crew near Seltzer Creek, not far from Avery, Idaho, realized that they were going to be trapped by the flames. One of the men, Oscar Weigert, pulled a pistol from his belt, put it to his head, and shot himself. It was a needless death. Just as the flames seemed about to engulf the crew, the wind shifted. All the remaining men were saved. Weigert too would have been safe.

Only a few miles away the story was different. The flames trapped a crew of twenty-eight men, who were all burned to death. Not one survived. Another crew of eighteen men on Big Creek met the same fate. Gale-force winds swept the fire over them. They never had a chance. Not one lived.

Weigle, who had been on the Wallace evacuation train, had further adventures. When the train stopped awhile, he met a man whose family, on a farm up in the hills, was in danger. The man was ill, so Weigle decided to help him. Weigle got off the train and went up to the small farm. He found that his own crew was already there, so he decided to walk back to the railroad and return to Wallace to give aid to the troops there.

As he was walking toward the tracks, a hurricane of wind blew the fire toward him. Weigle tried to outrun it, but the fire, moving with a howling moan, swept across his path. The flames seemed to be shooting out of a gigantic blowtorch. Weigle was in terrible danger and alone, but he knew the country well. There were many small mines in the hills. One was half a mile away, and Weigle headed for it. As he raced through the woods, so did the fire. At times the flames were literally at his heels. Had the wind shifted more toward him, he would have been killed.

When he got to the mine, he was surprised to see that another fire had gotten there first. The timbers holding up the inside of the mine shaft were in flames. Half the roof had caved in. The whole mine shaft was ready to collapse at any second. But there was water in the mine. It was either get trapped in the mine or burn to death.

Weigle ran inside the mine. He got to the water and drenched himself and his clothes. Then, his hat filled with water, he ran out. He found some loose sand. He quickly dug a shallow trench with his bare hands, hollowing out a place to put his head down and breathe. As he lay down, the full force of the flames hit him.

For a while his wet clothes withstood the flames. But they dried. He was becoming burned as flames see-sawed across his back. He wanted to scream or run, but he knew that if he lifted his head he would breathe in the flames. That would kill him outright.

Just when he felt that he was gone, the flames let up. He stayed in his trench until midnight. Then he looked around. The forest was glowing and filled with smoke, but he had lived. He stood up. Most of his burned clothes fell off of him. He started out for Wallace. He soon found that he could not follow the railroad anymore. The burned bridges stopped him. He walked by another route. He came to a wooden water pipe that carried water to Wallace. It was on fire. Though badly burned, mostly naked, and in pain, Weigle took the time to fill his hat with water from a nearby reservoir and single-handedly fought the fire on the pipe. He quenched the fire. Then he put his hat back on and doggedly walked on toward Wallace.

When people in the town saw Weigle walking toward them, they could hardly believe it. He looked more like a scarecrow than a human being. All the hair on his head and eyebrows had been burned off. His face was black. Only a few strips of clothing hung on him. His skin was burned. But tough Weigle lived on to a ripe old age!

Other dramas took place that same day.

During the worst of it, Ranger E. C. Pulaski, a descendant of Casimir Pulaski, the famous military commander who aided the Americans during the American Revolution, was heading a crew of 150 men on the high divide between the St. Joe and Coeur d'Alene rivers. The flames swept so swiftly over the area where he and his men were that part of his crew was separated from him. He tried to get to those men, but it was impossible. He had no idea whether they had survived or died.

Actually the men had run for it. At first they had no idea where to go. All around were flames, pushed toward them by high winds. To their amazement, they saw tree after tree explode into flames. They ran until they were backed up against a high pinnacle of rock. Looking up, they saw that its top soared above the fire. Could they climb it? It was steep enough to challenge an expert mountain climber. They had no choice but to try—it was that or burn to death. They started up as the flames raced toward them. They hoisted themselves and each other up. Time and again they seemed about to fall, but by some miracle they all reached the top. All around them was a sea of flame. If ever men looked into the face of hell, they did. Most of the time they lay on the rock with their faces down for protection from flying hot ashes. Without any source of water, they became dehydrated almost to the point of death. All of them ran high fevers. During the night the fire died down a bit. When they looked down they saw below them a forest lit by countless billions of sparks, glowing embers, and flaming trees. All the men on the rock lived.

Pulaski and his men were in worse danger. He, the remaining crew, and their two horses headed toward Wallace. But fire swept through the trees toward them. He saw that their route to Wallace was cut off by a huge wall of flame. Then he remembered that there was a mine about five miles away. It was their only hope. They went there as fast as they could. They were not quite fast enough. Just as they were reaching the mine, flames swept around them. One man died. Pulaski and the others, with the horses, made a dash to the mine and got into it. The mineshaft went back about one hundred feet. Fortunately there was water in it. Pulaski and the men wet down themselves and the horses. Because smoke was quickly filling the mine, Pulaski ordered the forty-one men to lie down. He himself took a wet blanket and held it in the mine entrance to bar the smoke. The blanket soon dried and burned. He held another ... and another. Each time the same thing happened. Pulaski's hands were blistered. After a while, there were no more blankets, and no way of keeping the flames out of the mine itself. One man, seeing the tongues of flame shoot into the mine, went almost insane with fear. He wanted to run out of the mine. Some tried to stop him, but he broke loose. Pulaski drew out a pistol and, aiming it at the man, told him to get into the back of the mine. He did so. All the men could do was to huddle as far away from the entrance as possible. They and the horses were trapped.

The fire outside howled and moaned and roared. Long flames reaching into the mine set the mine timbers ablaze. Pulaski, fearful that the timbers would go, took hatfuls of water, throwing it on the timbers. Men passed out from the heat and smoke. Pulaski himself staggered and collapsed unconscious onto the mine floor. Soon all but one man had become unconscious. Night fell. Slowly the raging fire began to die down. At midnight the only man who remained conscious crawled across the others, whom he was sure were all dead. He walked alone through the burning, charred forest to Wallace. It was a terrible and dangerous trip, but he made it. When the officials who had returned to Wallace heard of the remaining men in the mine, they sent out a rescue party.

When the rescue party arrived at the mine, they saw a dreadful sight. In the farthest back corner of the mine lay a heap of bodies. In its midst were two horses gasping and twitching in agony. The rescuers went in to take out the corpses. To their utter amazement and joy, they discovered that most of the men were alive. Only five were dead. Before leaving, the rescuers shot the horses to put them out of their misery.

Other crews were having equally harrowing times. Deputy Forest Supervisor Ed Thenon led a crew of firefighters near Moose Creek. Their job was to make fire trails, that is, to clear away trees and undergrowth in key places so that flames could be stopped.

During the day of the twelfth, none of them saw any fire.

Nevertheless, clouds of smoke and ash filled the air. At times they worked in smoke so thick that they could not see each other. That night they ate supper and went to sleep in a camp. Although Thenon was utterly exhausted from the day's work, he could not sleep. During the night he listened to the wind shifting in the trees. He heard pine needles falling on his tent. He had a feeling that something terrible was about to happen. And happen it did.

At about ten o'clock that night, flames traveling at express-train speeds roared toward the camp. Thenon jumped out of bed. The flames were so bright that it was almost like daylight. He woke up the crew. He ran to investigate a nearby creek. It was only eight feet wide and had a mere seven inches of water in it. It was not much, but it was all they had.

When Thenon got back into camp, the flames were almost upon them. He implored the men to hurry to the creek, but half of the thirty men in camp refused to go. They wanted to run for it. Thenon knew they would die if they tried to outrun the flames, but he could not force them to obey him. He jumped up on a stump and yelled to them, "Obey me and we'll live." Those who were going to run hesitated. Thenon walked to the creek, hoping they would follow him. They did. All the men gathered at the creek. They waited as the glowing wall of fire moved toward them out of the night.

Many were so frightened that they broke down. Some screamed. Others cried or prayed. At the last minute, some tried to run away, but their companions held them back. One man began to sing lullabys.

A blast of superheated air hit them. It swept in advance of the flames themselves. Thenon grabbed a bucket and put it over his head. He knew that a breath of that air would fatally sear his lungs. The bucket protected him. Even so, it was so intensely hot that he was sure he would die. Then the temperature suddenly dropped although flames were sweeping through the branches above them. Thenon, his eyes swollen from the heat, looked about. To his amazement, the men were still alive.

Soon the fire moved on and they all stood up. Thenon called roll. Two men were missing. Thenon was sure he had lost them. They must have run at the last minute and were now dead someplace in the forest. But a few minutes later the two men appeared. They walked toward the creek from the charred forest itself. The others could hardly believe it. The two explained that they had huddled in the dirt under the roots of a huge cedar tree. The flames never touched them.

Thenon had to be pleased. He and his men had been inside a blast furnace of heat and had all lived. The only sad note to the story is that the man who sang the lullyabys had lost his mind. Later he had to be placed in an insane asylum.

Within a few days the fire died down. The Forest Service started to search for and count the dead. Several dead crews were found. Oddly, one crew of seventeen men under Ranger Joe Helm could not be located at first, dead or alive. They were not discovered until almost a week after the fire. The men had survived on a sand bar in Bean Creek. Ill and fearing to move on because of the constant threat of fire, they had remained put until discovered.

This fierce fire, caused in part by lightning, had taken eighty-five lives. Seventy-eight firefighters died. In addition, three people had died near Newport, Washington, two in Wallace, one in Taft, and one at the St. Joe River.

A great many people were sent to hospitals. Most were burn patients. The worst of the burn injuries were to eyes and lungs.

The huge fire had destroyed over three million acres of land and millions of dollars' worth of valuable timber. The damage was so great that no timber whatsoever was taken out of the affected area until 1947, and that timber was of poor quality.

11. The 1930s Dust Bowl

It is not difficult to understand how droughts occur once you understand the earth's wind-flow patterns. The United States lies in what is termed the northern temperate zone. Circulating around the northern temperate zone are winds called the westerlies. They blow continually, always moving air from the west toward the east. Their influence on long-term weather trends is profound.

The westerlies snake around the northern hemisphere. They move like a twisting river of air across the continents and seas. They do not, however, follow a fixed course. The westerlies shift from year to year and from decade to decade—even from century to century—and as a result our weather patterns are never truly stable. The shifts in course can occasion long-term droughts or long wet spells. They may even prompt "little ice ages," those centuries when the northern hemisphere is so cold that ice clogs the harbors of Iceland and Greenland and glaciers grow larger in the mountains of Europe, North America, and Asia.

It is because the westerlies do not remain in a fixed position that varying weather patterns develop. It is now known, in part due to research done by Reid A. Bryson, professor of meteorology at the University of Wisconsin–Madison, that as the climate becomes colder, the westerlies gradually expand and move farther south. When that happens, they loop up and down across the northern hemisphere to such a degree that the loops may cause north or south winds to blow for decades in some places, even though the general trend of the loops is always from west to east. During warm periods, the westerlies shrink and move northward. When this happens, the loops are much less pronounced, and the winds stay much closer to a due west–to–due east position.

Bryson and his colleagues made an important discovery. When the climate is warm, the westerlies flow *around* the northern part of the Rockies. The winds then sweep down over the Great Plains. When this pattern holds, two things of importance happen. First, because the northern winds are moist, rains fall over the plains. Second, when the westerlies are so far north, moist air from the Gulf of Mexico can more easily move northward, bringing more moisture.

When the northern hemisphere is cool during a long spell lasting for decades, the westerlies move farther south as they expand. When that happens, they often blow over a more southern part of the Rocky Mountains. The winds also move with greater speed. This causes drought in the Great Plains.

There are reasons why this is so. First, as the west wind climbs up the Rocky Mountains' western slope, it is cooled and the moisture in it, carried there from the Pacific Ocean, condenses. Rain or snow falls from the clouds, covering the western slope of the Rockies with precipitation. The now-dry wind descending down the east slope of the mountains becomes warmer as it loses elevation. It warms up because the air at lower elevations is more compressed than it is at higher elevations, and this compression has a warming effect.

As the warm winds, called Chinooks, flow out over the Great Plains, they cause droughts. The faster the winds blow, the farther east the droughts will extend. When the winds hold that pattern for years, they cause severe droughts. These conditions are worsened by the fact that the westerlies, when they are so far south, block moisture-bearing winds coming north from the Gulf of Mexico.

Bryson wanted to research this expected pattern in depth. To do so, he and his workers did archeological work investigating the Mill Creek Indian culture of pre-Columbian northwest Iowa. Bryson was sure that if his ideas were correct, he would find signs in old Indian village sites that droughts had occurred in the past. His guess proved to be true. He and his workers dug up old villages and sifted through ancient garbage left by the Indians in mounds near their villages. By making note of evidence in the form of corncobs and seeds of various fruits and vegetables, as well as the bones of animals, Bryson and his group could chart and date the diet of the Indians. These investigations showed that during the years 1200–1400 A.D. there had been a severe drought in the region. As the drought progressed, plants needing a regular supply of moisture died off. Only drought-resistant plants remained. Animals became fewer. Finally the Indians left, moving out of the region.

The cause of the drought? The southerly westerlies. Also affecting the region were high winds coming over the Rockies that pushed the hot, dry air farther east than normal.

These finds changed previously held ideas about weather patterns over the Plains states. Until now, agricultural experts and other authorities had believed that the droughts of the 1930s were most likely caused by poor farming practices. This appears not to be the case. The droughts were caused by natural events.

Moreover, the 1930s drought was less severe by far than the hundred-year drought of the period from 1200 to 1400 A.D.

It should be pointed out that, during that long, severe drought, many regions to the west of the Rockies were receiving *more* moisture than usual. For two hundred years more rainfall and snow fell in the mountains. It is important to note this, for many people have the mistaken notion that there is such a thing as worldwide drought. There has never been a hint of such a thing. What happens is usually quite simple. When one place loses its yearly quota of rainfall, another place on earth receives more rainfall.

However, in spite of the fact that there had been severe droughts in the Plains states before the 1930s, the drought of that decade was, without a doubt, the worst that any white person had ever seen. Not only were vast amounts of sod blown away, but rivers were also lower than in any previous years. In terms of economic loss and human tragedy, the American dust storms of the 1930s have no equal. Of course, the fact that they hit the Midwest right in the very middle of the depression years only magnified their tragic consequences. They could not have arrived at a worse time. Moreover, the Dust Bowl had the most far-reaching economic, political, and social effects of any condition caused solely by weather in American history.

In spite of the fact that there had been terrifying dust storms in the 1890s, people seemed—as they always do—to have forgotten about them. From about 1900 until 1930 the Great Plains received more than their normal share of rainfall. Though one can never say even during the best of years that the plains look lush, they at least were amazingly productive. Huge fields of wheat covered thousands of square miles from the Canadian border into Texas. Wheat was blond gold. During World War I, it fed America and its allies. In the growing season, farm equipment was worked day after day, at times late into the night, plowing, planting, harvesting. Men, women, and children worked together on the farms. Their days were long and grueling, but at the end of each year they had a little more money. Up to the beginning of the 1930s, things were looking better all the time.

There were slums and sweatshops in the East. There were tenant farmers in the South. In effect there was a crescent of poverty halfway around the Midwest. Most people in the farm belt of the Midwest, from Canada to Texas and from Arkansas to Colorado, were not poor, certainly not poverty stricken. Comparatively speaking, they were well off. Most were farmers. Those who were not, directly depended upon them. The bankers, merchants, machinists, and others who served the farmers needed them. This was almost 100 percent, a farm economy, and the richest and best in the world.

Prosperity did not appear to be threatened. Oh yes, the farmers expected some years to be a little drier than others, but then other years would be wet enough to get things back to normal quickly again. In the long run, there seemed little reason for alarm.

In 1930—ironically the very first year of the Great Depression—the water level in the Mississippi River dropped drastically. People living along it were amazed. There were exposed mud flats where water had always flowed since anyone could recall. Underwater wrecks, long roots, and other objects never seen before lay exposed in the hot sun. The cause, of course, was simple. Lack of rain in the Plains states. By late summer, the mud flats were no longer mud flats. They were patches of dry, cracked earth as hard as concrete. No one had ever seen anything like it.

Meteorologists searched through old records. They shook their heads. No, nothing like it had every been reported. This was the worst drought on record.

How did it start? Did it begin as most writers say, because farmers broke the plains sod with steel plows that killed off the natural grasses and loosened the soil? Was it because farmers cut down so many trees that they allowed the winds a clean sweep of the land? Probably not. In spite of this commonly held belief, there is good evidence that points to a more basic cause: simply a lack of rain. The farmers may have worsened things, but the Dust Bowl was first and last a weather problem.

The dust clouds, called "rollers" because they appeared to roll across the plains, had been seen before the 1930s. In the 1890s, according to one writer of the time, the wind "just naturally blew and blew and blew and blowed and blowed and swept the country up in one great continuous sweep." He went on to write that nothing was safe and no one was sure of the outcome. We read from the *Johnson City* (Kansas) *Journal* in April 1895 that "the worst storm ever witnessed by our oldest residents passed over the western part of this country and eastern Colorado, April 5th and 6th. It was a combination of snow and sand, which was blown across the prairie at a terrific speed, uninterrupted for 40 hours. The Cimarron, North Fork, Little North Fork, San Arroyo, Horse Creek and Butte were strewn for miles with dead carcasses."

In Stanton County, Kansas, three children, ages eight to thirteen, were lost in that same storm and later found dead.

Old records show us that the Great Plains have always had dust storms. They scoured the plains long before steel plows dug into the earth to loosen the soil and long before the native plants were killed off and replaced by crops and imported grasses. All dust storms of the region have one cause—lack of rainfall. When the rain stops, the native (or imported) grasses dry up and die. Eventually their roots, which hold the soil, wither and decay. When that happens, nothing remains to hold the soil when the wind blows. Dust clouds form.

The year 1930 was a bad time for a drought. Because of the stock-market crash only months before, there were already bread lines and the first Hoovervilles. Now prosperous Midwest farmers were economically threatened. The drought spread. By the year's end, thirty states were feeling the effects. Three hundred counties of prime agricultural land were dry. One million farm families lived in the region.

There had been hints of economic trouble already. Prices for farm equipment in the late 1920s had risen so much that some farmers had gone bankrupt, while others abandoned their farms. Businesses in the area failed. So did some of the banks. Now there was a drought to top it all off. Things worsened rapidly. By the end of the year thousands of animals had died because farmers could not buy feed for them. Many families found themselves in desperate straits. Farmers began looking for supplemental incomes to feed their families.

Tempers quickly flared. In several places, such as Arkansas, white farmers shot at blacks who were working on highways and railroads to scare them away. The farmers wanted the jobs.

The drought spread even into the East. Police guarded water supplies in New Jersey "so no damned farmer could tap the pipes to water some stinkin' little corn field." Drinking water was actually sold in West Virginia.

President Herbert Hoover requested that railroad freight fees be cut. He reasoned that this would help farmers ship wheat and corn and also lower the price of fodder for their animals. The Interstate Commerce Commission cut the rate. This helped a good deal. Hoover also called together the governors of the Plains states to discuss further measures. Water was diverted from the Great Lakes to farming areas. Land on military reserves was opened up for cattle grazing. The Senate appropriated $60 million for emergency farm loans. Perversely, just as the bill went to the House of Representatives, Hoover said that the figure was too high, so the requested figure was cut to $25 million. Congressman John H. Garner, who would later be the vice-president of the United States of America, was furious. He said, "If it ever comes to a point where starving people must be taken care of, I will help take care of them, out of the treasury of the United States." After a struggle the bill went through for $45 million. In spite of this relief from the federal government, however, the situation in the country was getting worse. The farm disaster widened.

On January 3, 1931, an amazing event in American history took place. Five hundred heavily armed farmers and their wives invaded England, Arkansas. They marched to the office of the local American Red Cross chairman and quietly asked for food. The chairman glanced at the shotguns, rifles, and pistols nervously but firmly said, "No!"

The farmers said, "We're not beggars. We're willing to work, but we are not going to let our children starve." They went on to the town's food stores. The frightened store owners handed them flour and lard. Silently the people took the food and walked away. No shots had been fired by either the farmers or sheriffs.

This now almost forgotten news story was flashed all over the world, winning attention even from the Chinese and Japanese press. Dozens of articles were written about it. Plays based upon it were written and were acted in front of large audiences. A town in the richest nation on earth, the breadbasket of the world, had been invaded by farmers who demanded and were given food.

On January 31, 1931, there was a second such invasion of a city. A mob of five hundred hungry people marched to the Oklahoma City city hall. When their request for food was turned down, they stormed a store. Things quickly got ugly. This time there was a massive police counterattack. Fortunately, no one was killed; but all the men were taken to jail. The women were released and told to get moving fast.

The Red Cross began handing out ten cents a day for food to hungry people. But who could live on that, even in the early 1930s? In the very worst prisons, convicts were daily given

On September 14, 1930, a sandstorm heads toward Big Spring, Texas. "Rollers" like these plagued the Midwest during the dust bowl years. *Bradshaw/National Archives*

meals that cost twenty-nine cents a day. Free Americans were supposed to feed themselves for one-third the cost of feeding criminals. Relief workers handing out money said they often found a desperately hungry family that would refuse the handout. "We ain't so hungry, but down in them trees lives a family in a shack that is really starving" was a typical comment. Really starving? Many relief workers were staggered by such remarks, but they were often afraid to go down in the trees and hunt around for the hidden shack of a squatter family. Still, they knew that in hidden groves of trees were people starving to death. Dying of starvation in America! And the depression and drought were not even two years old.

In 1931 the dust clouds came. In 1932 they were worse. In 1934 they seemed to come from hell itself.

Hubert H. Humphrey, who would later become vice-president of the United States, was then living in Huron, South

Dakota. In 1931 he was planning to follow in his father's foot-steps and someday take over the family pharmacy. Then he saw the dust clouds. He wrote, "God, it was terrible . . . so hot, so terribly hot . . . the dust, it was everywhere. . . . You felt trapped." Humphrey actually became ill from the dust clouds. One day, as black dust clouds roared through Huron, he lost control and went on a rampage. He broke every glass in the store. Later he was hospitalized for severe stomach problems, which he later realized were brought on by the tension of con-tinually seeing the dust, tasting the dust, having the dust sift down his neck. Desperate, he gave up all ideas of taking over the family business and left Huron for good. Later he wrote, "I learned more about economics from one South Dakota dust storm than all my years in college."

The dust storms were awesome, and there was something unnatural about them. They often arrived as a moving wall of black, boiling, dry dust. These were the famous rollers. They defied explanation. The black dust, often either cold or burning hot, obliterated the landscape. One felt helpless in the face of a roller. When it swept across the land, the sun was darkened. The world became blacker and blacker. Even bright street lights could not cut through the gloom. And then one felt the grit of the dust on the teeth. What an awful sensation. It got in one's eyes and nose. It got in one's ears, mixing with the ear wax. It sifted down one's neck. It blew through buttonholes. It worked its way to one's privates.

On top of all that, the dry, static electricity accompanying the dust made people jumpy. U.S. Army reports on the effects of dust storms and dry air on troops in the Sahara Desert during World War II showed that this was not just a psychological effect. The electric charges had an actual physiological effect on one's nervous system. A person already at the point of want-ing to scream would scream. He'd be ready to fight everyone. He'd want to yell at others to leave him the hell alone.

There was no escape from the dust. No window could keep it

out, nor even the tightest-fitting door. During the worst of the storms, housewives draped their windows with wet sheets. They pounded wet rags into every crack. Did it help? Not much. Some housewives served meals in a peculiar fashion. To keep dust out of the food, they kept all the pots covered. Then they set the table and quickly covered all the plates with a large tablecloth. Again quickly, they took covered pots to the table and put them under the tablecloth. Then the family would gather. At a signal, each would lift part of the tablecloth, put his or her head under it, and eat his or her meal as fast as possible, before the dust ruined it.

Gordon Grice of Oklahoma used to take refuge in a wellhouse with his mother and the rest of the family. There they could escape the worst of the blowing dust. The wellhouse was lit by a candle. Once it went out, so Grice lit a match to relight the candle. To his surprise, he could actually see dust floating in the air and build up on the lighted match. He watched until the dust got so deep on the match that it put out the flame.

Another time he was leading mules through a dust storm. He could see neither the front feet of the mules nor his own feet. How did he know where to go? He felt the ground ahead for ruts with his feet. He knew where the ruts went, so he followed them.

The dust killed. Near Huron, two children walking home from school were overtaken by a roller. They soon became lost. From appearances, they wandered all afternoon and late into the night. Then they dropped from exhaustion and died. Their bodies were found partly buried under a layer of dust. National figures on deaths due to the dust seem impossible to come by, but scattered newspaper reports throughout the Plains states mention deaths of marooned automobile drivers, of farmers lost in their fields, and of children coming and going to school or working outdoors. The dust also greatly shortened the lives of people with weak lungs.

The winds blew so hard that dust dunes formed in many

areas. These could cover farm machinery and reach as high as the second floor of a house. They looked for all the world like snowdrifts, but they were brown and would never melt.

The sun beat down on a barren, desolate landscape. The air temperature often went over the hundred-degree mark. Soil temperatures about three inches under the ground reached a staggering 154° F. No wonder seeds of all types died. Most were roasted. Even had they sprouted, the heat alone would have killed them.

The dust clouds were so huge and widespread that they reached the East Coast. Several times dust fell on the platform of the Empire State Building. New Yorkers were amazed to look up and see dusty yellow skies above the city. Dust blew at least six hundred miles out to sea. Sailors mopping decks in the mid-Atlantic were surprised to see dirt from the Midwest on their decks. On April 2, 1935, senators gathered on the steps of the U.S. Capitol Building watched huge dust clouds rolling over Washington, D.C. The clouds were thick enough to darken the sun and turn the afternoon into a twilight gloom.

For most farmers, it was hopeless to hang on, in spite of the fact that many desperately wanted to stay in their home region. This was especially true of those who owned farms established by their homesteading ancestors. To give up was, for many, a heart-rending decision. But without crops to pay bills, farmers quickly went from moderate wealth to utter poverty. Many, fearing mortgage foreclosure, outwitted sheriffs for a while, hoping for better times. But better times did not come. The farmers finally had to leave. Others never waited to be evicted. They simply abandoned homes and farms.

The worst evil of the dust bowl was the widespread malnutrition it occasioned. Malnutrition and disease go hand in hand. During even the worst famines, few people actually die of starvation. Diseases kill the great majority of people first. They quickly die of illnesses that healthy people can usually just

In Curry County, New Mexico, dust covers a road. Such storms quickly formed dust dunes, which covered fields, roads, and even houses for miles around. *McLean/ National Archives*

shrug off—colds, stomach troubles, respiratory infections, etc. Infants in particular cannot fight off diseases when they are suffering from malnutrition. Hundreds of diseases that hardly affect a well-fed baby can kill an undernourished baby in a twinkling. In the afternoon a baby can appear to be relatively healthy. By next morning the infant is dead.

During the drought and depression, malnutrition was extensive. Poverty-stricken farmers and their families were forced to eat the worst of foods: sowbelly, flour, and a few pathetic greens. Barely fed, they had to take any job that they could. Skinny, skeletal-looking men worked long, hard hours in fields under a hot sun that roasted them in hundred-degree weather. Women weakened by lack of food nevertheless washed, cooked, and took care of hungry children. The mortality rate went up sharply. Farm families arriving in filthy, unsanitary migrant-worker camps, where raw sewage flowed in exposed ditches, walked into the teeth of death. The children came down sick, usually with fatal diarrhea. The old men coughed themselves to death. Women died of fevers.

In 1934 tenant farmers and sharecroppers in Arkansas formed the Southern Tenant Farmers Union. Landowners, fearing that some of their profits might be lessened, paid local sheriffs and police to break up the union. In a travesty of justice, the official representatives of the law flogged union members, lynched many, and systematically burned down their cabins. They even had the audacity to ride the Socialist candidate for president, Norman Thomas, out of town on a rail. Thomas was outraged, to say the least. He asked for and obtained a meeting with Franklin Roosevelt. To Thomas's complaints President Roosevelt soothingly replied, "We've got to be patient."

Roosevelt decided that, instead of trying to aid the plains farmers in their own states, it would be much better to resettle them on more productive farmlands. The Farm Security Administration was set up with this goal in mind. It planned to aid a half million farmers, but in the end it lacked funds and was only able to help forty-five hundred. Its accomplishments were minimal.

Congress next decided to raise food prices so that farmers would receive more for their crops. They set up the Agricultural Assistance Administration (AAA). It paid farmers not to grow crops on their land. With fewer farm goods on the market, prices, because of the law of supply and demand, should rise. The whole idea of the program was to help Dust Bowl farmers.

To receive the money, there was a catch. The farmer had to own his land. Because of this ruling, the AAA unwittingly brought about a new tragedy. Southern landowners took the money, and since they were no longer going to raise crops, they threw sharecroppers and tenant farmers off their land. These people, who had always been at the bottom of the economic scale, were now in even worse shape. Not knowing where to go or what to do, they drifted about. In most cases, income was less than $200 a year per family. Of course, they never saw a cent of the cash. The landowners took all their money to pay off debts incurred in the struggle for survival. Tenants were less than slaves. Slaves at least had value, but these people had none. Many were reduced to eating weeds. Pellegra, malaria, and malnutrition had them dying off like flies—their death rate was fantastically high. What bitter irony. A government program substantially designed to aid Dust Bowl farmers had the effect of killing off southern sharecroppers and tenant farmers both black and white. The fatal force of the drought was supplemented by man in a strange, convoluted sort of way.

The Dust Bowl played a major role in spurring the population growth of states to the west, especially California. Under yellow, dust-filled skies, weary farmers headed west in jalopies. They crossed the dried-out, defeated plains in their tin lizzies, with mattresses tied by clothesline to the car tops. In each car could be seen the sad faces of the children, the broken looks of the wives and mothers, the sunken, gone faces of the men. Death traveled with them. Disease was rampant; the mortality rate was high.

As they fled, the great clouds of dust continued to move in the howling wind. The horizon disappeared in a sickly yellow haze. The hot sun beat down. Along the roadside stood farmhouses, broken and empty to the wind. Farm equipment rusted and became buried in sand. Green, succulent leaves had withered to brittle brown tissue paper. Dunes of soft, powderlike

dust marched across dead fields. On freight trains jerking west-
ward, weary, dust-covered men hitched rides to a hoped-for new
start.

And so they moved—at first by the dozens, then by the
hundreds, then by the thousands, all leaving the Dust Bowl. Few
journeys were so painful. Cars broke down along the way. Rip-
off artists waited in every little town. At night the refugees—
for so they were— surreptitiously buried their dead along the
highways. And still they came, swarms of them, frightened,
angered, and finally and worst of all, despondent, unable even
to think or to feel. Along the way sheriffs, scabs, strike breakers,
and others jailed them, beat them up, humiliated them. Others
profited from them: bar owners, sleazy motel keepers, and at
the end of the line, California landowners, who now had so
much cheap labor that they could make unprecedented profits.

The only life form to flourish during the droughts was the
locust. On fluttering wings they appear as huge black clouds
over a farmer's field and eat it to the ground in minutes. During
the Dust Bowl years, many farmers who had managed margin-
ally to survive the drought and dust clouds lost their holdings
because of the locusts.

Under Franklin Roosevelt's direction, the government tried
once more to save the farmers of the Dust Bowl. The Civilian
Conservation Corps (CCC) was sent into the region. Key rivers
and erosion-causing streams were dammed. These dams held
water from precipitation runoff, which gave moisture enough
time to seep into the ground. If it had not been for the dams,
precious water would have raced downstream to rivers and to
the sea, without aiding the land at all. But the Plains states are
huge in area and the dams that were built were relatively few
and far between. To stop the howling winds from tearing away
more topsoil, Roosevelt also insisted that a shelter belt of trees
be planted in the region. Many scoffed at the idea. Trees would
never grow in such dry country, and it was a waste of time to

even make the attempt, they declared. Roosevelt, however, got his way, and the CCC planted the trees. Two hundred million trees were planted. A huge shelter belt one thousand miles long and a hundred miles wide was planted. Did these massive, heroic programs help? It is difficult to say. By the time the trees began to mature, the drought had been broken by the rains, which had finally returned.

When the real, long-term rains came, as they finally did in 1937, they came quickly and fully. To the joy of the inhabitants of the Plains, in the spring of 1937 huge dark clouds piled up in the sky—not rollers, not dusters, but rain clouds. Lightning forked out of them. So too came the wonderful song of thunder. People stood in fields with their arms outstretched as cold torrents of rain soaked them to the skin. They were saved. The Plains states—the very states that had suffered the most—had a miraculous recovery to become, once more, the breadbasket of the world. Thanks to that rich land, its people, and the rains, Americans, Spanish, Chinese, Russians, Israelis, Nigerians, Indians and others eat their daily bread.

12. The North African Sahel Drought

One of the most devastating catastrophes of the recent past was the drought of 1968–75 in North Africa. Nothing in modern times has equaled it. Floods, typhoons, and other natural disasters have killed large numbers of people, but in terms of deaths, lingering disease, malnutrition, social upheaval, displaced persons, and complete population shifts, this African drought was by far the worst natural disaster in the twentieth century.

The drought took place in the Sahel. In Arabic, *sahel* means shore or boundary. The African Sahel is a very large area of land bordering the southern rim of the Sahara Desert. The precise limits of the Sahel are vaguely defined. In general it is the low grass country that more or less parallels the area between 14°N and 18°N across Africa. It goes through Mauritania, Senegal, Mali, Niger, Chad, Sudan, Ethiopia, and Somalia. Though dry and usually supporting only scrubby brush, this land is not true desert. During good years, it is just fertile enough to support camels, sheep, goats, donkeys, and cattle in the north near the Sahara and, farther south, to allow farmers to grow millet and sorghum. Everywhere it is a hardscrabble place to live, even during the best of times. Yet it has a population of 25 million people—Tuareg, Flani, and other nomads; Arabs; blacks; and a few whites. North of the Sahel lies the huge, barren Sahara Desert, covering an area larger than the forty-eight contiguous states of the United States of America. South of the Sahel the land becomes richer, merging eventually into dense jungle.

During normal years the Sahel gets between fourteen and twenty-three inches of rain a year. These rains fall in brief downpours lasting less than an hour, primarily during the months of June and July. In many ways the rainfall patterns are like those found in the American Southwest. There is just enough rainfall for scrubby plants to grow, and these feed the people's herds and water their gardens.

The westerlies, which influence droughts in the American Great Plains, also influence droughts in India and northern Africa. They do this by pushing the monsoon winds that normally bring moisture to those regions out of the way. In the case of droughts in northern Africa, the westerlies push the needed monsoon rains too far south.

The monsoons, which usually dump some rain on the Sahel, carry moisture from the Atlantic Ocean in the huge baylike region south of Liberia, the Ivory Coast, Ghana, and Nigeria. During the summer the deserts heat up. As they do, the air rises. Cooler, heavier, but damper air from the Atlantic moves inland from the southwest to replace that rising air. This moist air brings rain. However, the westerlies can, if they are far enough south, keep monsoon winds from reaching either the Sahel or the Sahara. In that case equatorial Africa gets more rain, while the Sahel and areas farther north remain dry.

Economically, the Sahel is one of the poorest regions on

earth. People earn less than an average of $150 per year. It has, even in the best years, a very high annual death rate— over twenty-five people per thousand.

In spite of their poverty, before the drought most of the people were among the freest on earth. Many were nomads, as their ancestors had been since time immemorial. Families wandered from place to place with their herds. Unhindered by fences or national boundaries, they were able to camp under the stars at night and move on at will during the day. Since few ever went to school, paid taxes, or had anything to do with government, they lived out their lives as they saw fit. In former times, many were fierce bandits and raiders who fought off the Foreign Legion. These were people with a colorful past.

A drought, by its very nature, cannot begin swiftly. Sometimes it takes months, even years, to know that one is in progress. The great Sahel drought is usually dated as beginning in the summer of 1968. During the rainy season that year, only about half as much rain as normal fell over the whole region. Of course the rainfall varied from place to place, but no part of the Sahel got more rain than normal during 1968.

The people of the region had seen many dry years come and go. They were not too worried. Nevertheless, problems appeared that first year. Crops dwindled. Some failed all together. To the north, near the Sahara, things became bad more quickly, for it is always drier there. Winds began to blow sand over fields as the actual desert moved southward. Farmers planted crops several times in 1968, hoping that at least one of them would survive. Few did. Nomads, finding the more northern pastures parched, moved southward.

In 1969 things got worse. The summer temperatures, always hot, became roasting. For weeks on end the temperatures would soar above 120°F. Even streams that had always had some water in them dried up and disappeared. Sandstorms became more common. Nomads huddled in their tents while the winds howled and dust and sand swirled around them.

By the summer of 1970 it was evident that one of the worst droughts in memory was in progress. In Chad, half of the country's agricultural land lay buried under sand. Discouraged farmers abandoned their plots; nomads prodded their weary herds on ever longer treks in search of water. Many times nomads would head for rivers only to find huge sand dunes now filling the riverbeds. Often their only hope of finding water for their thirsty animals was to dig wells. When they got a well dug and water finally appeared, they would have to stay near the well for days. But this posed a serious problem. If the nomads stayed too long near a well, their animals would eat all the vegetation for miles around. Once that happened, though the animals might get water, they would get no feed. Then there was nothing to do but move on with the search for water someplace else, anyplace. Cattle soon looked like walking skeletons covered with loose skin. Pained by thirst, they lowed piteously. Everywhere one could hear the moaning of livestock. Even the sturdy camels suffered. Their proud humps became flabby. Desperate, the animals ate thorn trees and bark in an effort to survive. The Sahara moved even farther south. Under the impact of the heat and dryness, the land turned to sand, pebbles, and barren rocks.

Scientists have known for a long time that the Sahara Desert has been growing larger with each passing century. About thirty thousand years ago the region was lush. There were deep grasses, open forest land, and several large lakes and rivers. Early bushmen then living in the region had drawn pictures on Saharan rocks showing many animals, including the hippopotamus, that could never live in the desert today. But for thousand of years the region has progressively dried out and spread southward. Some years it stayed put. But by 1970 the desert was racing southward in some places at a rate of about thirty miles per year. The situation was desperate. This was especially so, because desert lands rarely if ever become fertile again.

After three years of drought, the entire economy of the Sahel began to collapse. Because of crop failures, farmers left their plots and went south to seek employment in cities where there were hardly any jobs. Moreover, the cities' prosperity often depended upon farm goods to buy and sell. Because of the drought, many merchants were already ruined.

The nomads were in particularly bad shape. They depended upon the meat and milk of their herds to feed themselves. Some lived almost exclusively on meat, milk, and often blood taken from their animals. But the animals were becoming weak and sickly. Milk became especially scarce. Slaughtered animals provided less and much poorer meat, so more animals had to be killed. Some nomads traditionally stuck tubes into the veins of living animals in order to drink the blood. In normal years this did not harm the animals. They had enough blood both for themselves and their masters. No longer. Furthermore, during normal times, the nomads could sell livestock to get vegetables and needed commodities. But scrawny, starving cattle were next to worthless. No one wanted to buy them.

Knowing that there was never enough grass and water at any one place for large herds, the nomads split them up. Different family members took the smaller herds to hunt for better pasture. This strategy split families. Brothers, sisters, husbands, and wives went their separate ways. Unfortunately, as time went on and conditions grew much worse, many became so poverty-stricken that they could not get back to their families. Moreover, as millions of people drifted back and forth through the immense Sahel, they had no idea where their lost loved ones might be. The drought broke up thousands of nomad families.

Farm families also broke up. Farmers abandoning their land to look for jobs in cities or heading south toward more fertile lands could not afford to take their families with them. They left promising to return with money or when things got better. Numerous villages were filled with farmers' wives and children waiting, waiting for men who never returned.

By 1971 Africa south of the Sahara was in social turmoil. Old

Millions of cattle perished in the Sahel during the drought of 1969–74. *United Nations/FAO/Botts*

ways of life were quickly breaking down, most notably the nomadic way of life. Farmers had fled their land. Cities were packed with poverty-stricken people.

By now nomads had almost no chance of producing wells or pasture for their animals. Often in looking for water and grass, the animals would be walked to death. The poor beasts would die, exhausted and dehydrated. Throughout the Sahel people could see carcasses of dead animals almost anywhere. If a nomad was lucky, his animals might die in a place where he could sell the hide. If so, he would haggle for hours with a trader over a few cents.

By the early 1970s almost all nomads and farmers in the Sahel were suffering from malnutrition. So were many city dwellers. The worst off were the elderly and infants. Many nomads with herds had to leave grandparents behind, as they and the children moved on with the animals. They would leave the old people in the shade of a tree, a jug of water and some bread beside them. Then sadly the rest of the family would move on. As they disappeared over the horizon, the old sat under the tree and waited for death.

Infants suffered the most. Hungry mothers had little or no milk in their breasts, and diseases quickly killed off the babies.

It took the world at large a long time to realize how desperate the situation in the Sahel really was. Of course, there were many reasons for this. Some were strictly political. Some governments did not want to broadcast their helplessness. There was, from their point of view, no need to let other countries know how defenseless they were, how badly things might appear to be managed. Other governments were wary of asking for food from Europe or America. They knew that food supplies often ended up in black markets to make the worst sectors of society rich. But most of all, almost everyone expected the rains to return soon. After all, droughts do end. None last forever, and as this one had been much longer than most, it should come to an end soon.

But the drought did not end. Things steadily worsened.

People who should have been in the prime of their life were dying. It was no longer just the elderly and infants. Death stalked everyone. Everywhere there were carcasses of dead animals, but now human corpses were seen too, many of teenagers and people in their twenties and thirties.

As always, the drought was worst in the north. Nomads who still had herds moved them ever farther south. But as the animals went south, they began to break through fences and trample on the crops of farmers also desperately trying to hang on to life. Many bitter fights broke out. Skeletal men fought skeletal men. All too often a dagger settled the final score.

The breakup of society increased. More and more families were separated. Nomads and farmers fought each other. In the crowded cities honest men were reduced to crime. Proud Tuareg women who had actually been the economic power in their tribes were forced into prostitution. Civil war threatened. In Ethiopia it was really the drought that toppled Haile Selassie. Most governments were paralyzed. At no level of the economy did anything work correctly. On top of all, the death toll rose continuously. This was a drought of biblical proportions.

Thousands of nomads who had lost their herds saw no reason to keep wandering. They headed for towns and cities such as Niamey, Niger; Timbuktu, Mali; Kiffa, Mauritania; Gao, Mali; and many other such places. The cities could not handle them. There was nothing to do with them but put them in refugee camps. For thousands this was the final death sentence. No matter how hellish it was out in the lonely desert and scrub country, it was at least clean. Sanitation was simple. Moreover, the hot, dry air and brilliant sun rays killed viruses and bacteria. In the filthy refugee camps, with open sewage and people crowding together, diseases spread rapidly.

The camps became hellholes. Thousands of weary, vacant-eyed people sat listlessly all day long, waiting for handouts of food. They had nothing to do. Many simply died of sadness.

Those who lived, especially children, were not in good shape. A British journalist said that *all* the children he saw in large refugee camps were deformed, and suffered from severe speech defects and lack of muscular coordination.

Most mornings trucks would come into the camps to pick up those who had died the night before. Sometimes not even that happened. Claire Sterling of the *Washington Post* reported that in one camp she visited, some children stood by their dead mother for three days, waiting for her to wake up.

Hospitals sprang up here and there. Most were run by churches and religious groups. Conditions were so critical that the doctors and nurses had to set up a system of priority treatment. Those suffering the most and who had the least chance of recovery were left to die. All the medical care was given to those who might recover and be able to resume a normal life.

By 1973 the world was finally aware that a terrible disaster of unprecedented proportions had befallen the region. By then the death toll was in the tens of thousands. Most of the Sahel's population suffered from malnutrition and disease. Millions of head of livestock were dead. The economy of the region had collapsed.

France and the United States sent in rescue teams, as did other countries, the United Nations, and many church organizations. Jacques Bugnicourt, who was on a United Nations international research team, interviewed several survivors.

A chief from Agadez, Niger, told him, "If we were near a village and we heard the sound of grain being ground, we sent the children to beg for the bran left behind after the grinding. The children would eat it on the spot, but had difficulty digesting it. If any was left, they would bring it back to us."

Bugnicourt was told that near Zinder a herdsman had thrown his wife and their two children down a well so as not to have to watch them die before his eyes.

In Gao, Mali, a nomad family told him, "There were eighteen of us to start with: six died on the way. . . . They were children who were used to drinking milk, but while we were traveling, they had nothing to eat but millet bran, and they suffered from stomachaches which finished them off."

Bugnicourt spoke with Hama, a fourteen-year-old boy from Timbuktu, Mali, who had become the head of a family of six members: himself, a woman twenty-five years of age, and four children. None of the others had survived. He said, "We set off on foot to escape from the drought-stricken area in March 1973. Two months later our little group was completely exhausted. Two boys, Moma and Mohamed, died, followed by five girls: Mariama, Asmao, Amintou, Aisha, and another Mariama."

The head of another family said, "The camels became too weak to carry us. We went on foot. Our old father was lagging behind and was slowing us up. Finally he sat down in the sand and told us he would catch up later. That same night my younger brother could stand it no longer and turned back to look for him. We have not seen my brother since. He must have got lost as well."

Stories of family separations were common. Another nomad told Bugnicourt, "We have no way of getting back to those who were left behind, and they have no means of coming here, nor of surviving back there where there is no livestock."

Interestingly, several revealed their dreams. One said that he "dreamed only of famine." Others in a refugee camp said they dreamed only of "the lorry [truck] which comes to distribute food." Others, however, dreamed of the lands where they had always lived. They dreamed "of having our animals and of living in the bush as we used to."

A few told of how their ancient customs had been changed by the drought. One said, "Before I only gave my daughters in marriage to Muslims. Now I would marry my daughters to anyone who brought us food."

By 1973 aid was being stepped up. In that year, the United States sent over 256,000 tons of grain to the region. Other countries sent over 369,000 tons of grain, for a total of 626,000 tons.

But sending the grain and getting it to the starving people were two completely different stories. It was quite easy to get grain to the large cities. But from that point on, problems mounted rapidly. In some places the grain never got off the docks. In Dakar food sat on the docks from July to November. Rains soaked it, and it fermented and rotted. Thousands of rats scampered over it. Few of the starving ever received a mouthful.

Much of the food went directly into the black market. Numerous crooks in back alleys at refugee camps became wealthy. So did many politicians. Moreover, those who got control over the black-market food had unbelievable power over the rest of the population.

Yet in the end the worst problem was transportation. The Sahel is an enormous, lonely place. Take Mauritania, for example. It is 397,950 square miles in size, half again as large as Texas. In all of Mauritania there were only 100 miles of paved road. Most of the starving people who needed food were scattered far and wide out in the bush country. How could anyone ever get food to them? Air drops and a few other attempts were made, but most failed. The place was too huge.

The only realistic way for people to get the food was to walk out of the bush country and go to various key cities. This sounds reasonable, but actually most people who desperately needed food were too weak to make the journey. But what could they do? Weak or not, they had to make the attempt. Many who might have survived by saving their strength and staying put actually walked themselves to death.

In spite of the fact that a good deal of food was getting through in some places, the death toll continued to rise steeply. Diseases spread through the region. Most people were extraordinarily susceptible to them in their weakened condition. Mea-

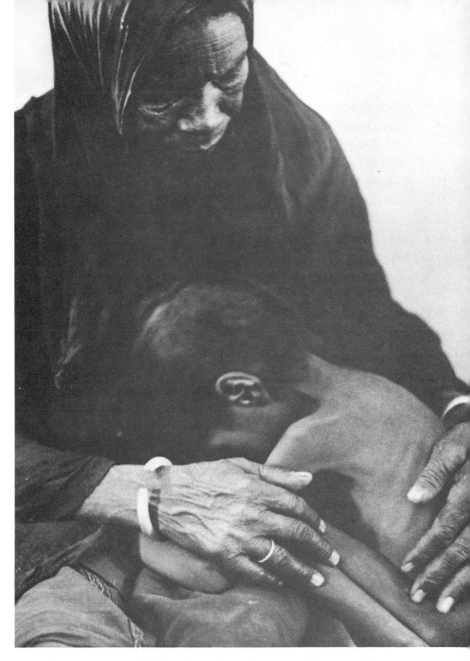

A woman at a hospital at Agadez near Niamey, Niger, comforts a child suffering from malnutrition. *United Nations/Gamma*

sles alone killed thousands of children. Diphtheria became rampant in many areas. Doctors rushing into the area inoculated thousands. Some tribal chiefs in Chad refused vaccines for diphtheria from relief organizations. They felt it was better for children to die of diphtheria than of starvation. They saw diphtheria as a blessing. It killed swiftly, whereas starvation was slow and painful.

No one knows how many people died, but by 1974 the death toll was staggering. The drought was at its worst. The Senegal River, for example, had dried to the extent that its waters could no longer carry away the salt that constantly got into the river. During normal years this salt would be so diluted that it was not even noticeable to humans and animals. By 1974, however, the river water was undrinkable, and yet livestock had nothing else to drink. In many places the river was choked with dead animals in piles that formed temporary dams. These backed up fetid, slimy, disease-ridden ponds. By 1974 at least 50 percent of all the herd animals had died. In many places over 80 percent were dead.

In 1975 the rains returned to the land. Unfortunately, they came with a vengeance. Some of the heaviest rains ever seen in the region fell on the parched land. Because the soil was so hard, the waters raced off of it. Since no plants held back the water, floods stripped many areas of valuable topsoil. Thousands of acres of land were ruined. Furthermore, the floodwaters carried tons of sand and dirt that filled in numerous wells, ruining them.

Farmers could not even take advantage of the damp soil, for they had been forced to eat seeds usually reserved for planting new crops.

Many wild plants did thrive, but huge packs of rats raced through the countryside eating everything in sight. Cats and dogs that might have kept the rat population down had gone into stew kettles long ago. Natural predators were dead. With nothing to stop them, the rats became kings of the Sahel.

It is probable that neither the Sahel nor its people will ever fully recover from the drought. The Tuareg, for example, were broken as a nomadic people by it. Dispersed, forced into city jobs, their way of life was over, their feudal system a thing of the past. The Sahara had advanced into much of the Sahel, and that area may never revert to scrub lands again, instead remaining forever sandy or rocky desert. The economic upheavals turned both social and political systems upside down. Those who survived the drought will never be the same. Most have now taken up a different way of life, have completely changed their life-style.

No one knows how many died in the drought. Estimates run from about one to two hundred thousand people. But this figure does not include thousands upon thousands of brain-damaged children or people crippled, weakened, and deformed by their suffering. A large part of the population still suffers psychological damage. This is true for the many who lost their families and for others who, once prosperous, were reduced to abject poverty and shame. The total damage was so great that there is no way of measuring it.

Some experts feel that this African drought might be a harbinger of things to come, not only in so-called Third World countries, but in the most advanced nations. A major drought in America, Europe, or Russia could bring about social and economic changes that would have devastating effects upon the whole world. Whether we like it or not, we are, all of us, dependent upon the rain that falls on wheat fields, the water in the rice paddies, and the summer showers that water the corn belt. The worst killer weather is a drought. This can occur almost anywhere. None of us can realistically ever feel completely safe.

Bibliography

Allen, Everett. *A Wind to Shake the World*. Boston: Little, Brown and Co., 1976.

Battan, Louis. *Weather*. Englewood Cliffs: Prentice-Hall, 1974.

Boonifield, Paul. *The Dust Bowl*. Albuquerque: University of New Mexico Press, 1979.

Briggs, Peter. *Rampage*. New York: David McKay Co., 1973.

Brown, Slater. *World of the Winds*. New York: The Bobbs-Merrill Co., 1961.

Bryson, Reid A., and Murray, Thomas J. *Climates of Hunger*. Madison: University of Wisconsin Press, 1977.

Butler, Hal. *Nature at War*. Chicago: Henry Regnery, 1976.

Clarke, Thurston. *The Last Caravan*. New York: G. P. Putnam's Sons, 1978.

Crawford, William P. *Mariner's Weather.* New York: W. W. Norton and Co., 1978.

Ellis, Deward Robb. *A Nation in Torment.* New York: Coward, McCann, 1970.

Encyclopedia Brittanica. Numerous articles on weather and climate.

Goldston, Robert. *The Great Depression.* New York: The Bobbs-Merrill Co., 1968.

Greeley, William B. *Forests and Men.* New York: Doubleday and Co., 1951.

Herber, Lewis. *Crisis in Our Cities.* Englewood Cliffs: Prentice-Hall, 1965.

Hoehling, A. A. *Disaster.* New York: Hawthorn Books, 1973.

Hoffer, William. *Saved: The Story of Andrea Doria.* New York: Summit Books, 1979.

Holbrook, S. H. *Burning an Empire.* New York: Macmillan, 1943.

Kimble, George H. T. *Our American Weather.* New York: McGraw-Hill, 1955.

Laffoon, Polk, IV. *Tornado: The Killer Tornado That Blasted Xenia, Ohio, in April, 1974.* New York: Harper & Row, 1975.

Lehr, Paul. *Weather.* Golden Press, 1957.

Lewis, Howard R. *With Every Breath You Take.* New York: Crown Publishers, 1965.

Mason, Herbert M., Jr. *Death from the Sea: Our Greatest Natural Disaster.* New York: The Dial Press, 1972.

Mills, Clarence A. *Air Pollution and Community Health.* Boston: The Cristopher Publishing House, 1951.

Monkhouse, F. J. *Principles of Physical Geography*. Totowa, N.J.: Littlefield, Adams and Co., 1966.

National Oceanic and Atmospheric Administration. *Tornado: Safety Rules in Schools* (NOAA/PA 74025). Washington: United States Government Printing Office.

————. *Thunderstorms*. (NOAA/PA 75009). Washington: United States Government Printing Office.

————. *Skywarn* (NOAA/PA 76019). Washington: United States Government Printing Office.

New Columbia Encyclopedia. Numerous articles.

New York Times. Numerous articles.

Rouche, Berton. *Eleven Blue Men*. Boston: Little, Brown and Co., 1953.

Sterling, Claire. "Calamity of Biblical Proportions." *Reader's Digest,* June 1974.

Stommel, Henry, and Stommel, Elizabeth. "The Year without a Summer." *Scientific American*. June 1979.

Thompson, Philip D., O'Brien, Robert, and the Editors of *Life*. *Weather* (Life Science Library). New York: Time Inc., 1965.

Tufty, Barbara. *1001 Questions Answered about Storms*. New York: Dodd, Mead & Co., 1970 .

UNESCO COURIER. August, 1973.

UNESCO COURIER. April 1975.

United States Department of Commerce. *American Weather Stories*. Washington: United States Government Printing Office.

Index